Making Space for What Matters

Find Freedom from Clutter & Hoarding with Acceptance & Commitment Therapy

JENNIFER KRAFFT, PHD
CLARISSA W. ONG, PHD
MICHAEL E. LEVIN, PHD
MICHAEL P. TWOHIG, PHD

New Harbinger Publications, Inc.

Publisher's Note

This publication is designed to provide accurate and authoritative information in regard to the subject matter covered. It is sold with the understanding that the publisher is not engaged in rendering psychological, financial, legal, or other professional services. If expert assistance or counseling is needed, the services of a competent professional should be sought.

NEW HARBINGER PUBLICATIONS is a registered trademark of New Harbinger Publications, Inc.

New Harbinger Publications is an employee-owned company.

New Harbinger Publications, Inc.
5720 Shattuck Avenue
Oakland, CA 94609
www.newharbinger.com

Cover design by Sara Christian

Acquired by Elizabeth Hollis Hansen

Edited by Amber Williams

Library of Congress Cataloging-in-Publication Data on file

Printed in the United States of America

27 26 25

10 9 8 7 6 5 4 3 2 1 First Printing

"Smart, sincere, and seriously helpful, this book offers a fresh, acceptance and commitment therapy (ACT)-based approach for people stuck in clutter and hoarding struggles. The authors—brilliant and big-hearted—translate solid science into real-world wisdom with clarity and compassion. If you're looking for a values-driven way forward that honors the messiness of being human, this book delivers."

—**D.J. Moran, PhD, BCBA-D**, associate professor at Touro University California, and featured psychologist on *Hoarding: Buried Alive* and *Confessions: Animal Hoarding*

"People with hoarding problems often feel imprisoned by their circumstances. In this book, Krafft, Ong, Levin, and Twohig describe a program that unlocks that prison. The key lies in understanding the meaning of possessions and their connection to life values. By guiding you to articulate these values and evaluate possessions in light of them, this program will help with decluttering and make your life more satisfying and fulfilled."

—**Randy O. Frost, PhD**, professor emeritus of psychology at Smith College, and author of *Stuff*

"The authors thoughtfully turn their years of valuable research and clinical experience into a friendly and digestible guide. Open this book. You'll find a compassionate and wise friend who gets you and is committed to walk alongside you, step by step, through the sometimes overwhelming and lonely journey of healing. I am really glad this book has been brought to the world!"

—**Chia-Ying Chou, PhD,** director of The San Francisco Center for Compassion-Focused Therapies, and the Better Treatment for Hoarding program

"*Making Space for What Matters* is a must-read book for anyone who's struggling with clutter overtaking their lives. Chock-full of practical exercises and examples, this rich resource is sure to help countless people live a more clutter-free life using state-of-the-art techniques and tools. If you're struggling with clutter or hoarding, this book is an excellent place to start. I'll be recommending it strongly to anyone looking to take the brave step of fighting their clutter or hoarding."

—**Greg Chasson, PhD, ABPP**, psychologist, associate professor of adult psychiatry at the University of Chicago, and coauthor of *Hoarding Disorder*

"As someone who researched hoarding and ACT for my PhD years ago, I've been waiting for exactly this book. Krafft, Ong, Levin, and Twohig have created a compassionate, research-backed guide that goes beyond organizing tips to address what's really happening beneath the clutter. I've used these principles with clients for years—they work. Finally, a practical resource that treats hoarding with the understanding it deserves."

—**Jan Eppingstall, PhD**, founder of Stuffology Consulting

"This book is a truly compassionate and evidence-based guide for anyone struggling with hoarding and cluttering behaviors. Drawing on ACT, all chapters go beyond traditional messages and tap into the core psychological processes that often accompany hoarding and cluttering. Page by page, this manuscript offers readers a clear path to living more freely and in alignment with their deepest values. A must-read!"

—**Patricia E. Zurita Ona, PsyD,** author of *The ACT Workbook for the Anxious Procrastinator*

We dedicate this book to everyone whose life has been impacted by hoarding or severe clutter. People with hoarding problems often feel deeply alone. We hope this book communicates that you are not alone and that a life with more room for meaning, purpose, vitality, and joy is possible for you.

Contents

Foreword

For many years, hoarding behaviors were a diagnostic anomaly. Some clinicians thought of it as a variant of obsessive-compulsive disorder (OCD), while the fourth edition of the *Diagnostic and Statistical Manual of Mental Disorders* (DSM-IV) listed hoarding only as a symptom of obsessive-compulsive personality disorder (OCPD). As research accumulated on hoarding, thanks in large part to the efforts of Drs. Randy Frost and Gail Steketee, it became clear that although some people can have multiple concerns, hoarding really didn't resemble OCD or OCPD in a meaningful way. It was not until the 2013 publication of the *DSM-5* that hoarding disorder (HD) became a formal diagnosis. That means we are well behind the curve in understanding what HD is about, where it comes from, and how best to treat it.

Several theoretical models of HD have been suggested. Frost's *cognitive-behavioral model* posits that hoarding stems from information-processing deficits, problems of emotional attachment, avoidance of decision-making, and maladaptive or exaggerated beliefs about possessions. Tolin's *biopsychosocial model* expanded on the cognitive-behavioral model, using recent neuroscience data to suggest that hoarding is characterized by a two-phase abnormality in brain function; in particular, areas of the brain that are responsible for determining the salience or relevance of situations are under-engaged at rest (which may help us understand the motivational issues often seen in HD) and over-engaged when having to make a personally relevant decision (so that the brain is saying that "everything is important"). Mathes's *attachment model* focuses on attachment anxiety (characterized by negative self-evaluation and fears of abandonment) and attachment avoidance (characterized by negative views of others and a subsequent desire to avoid social connection and intimacy). The attachment model of HD suggests that people with HD have thwarted interpersonal needs and compensate by attempting to form secure attachments with possessions.

So far, efforts to treat HD have been modestly successful. Though no medications have been proven to be efficacious for HD, *cognitive behavioral therapy* (CBT) has such evidence. Specifically, multiple well-controlled trials have demonstrated that CBT produces reliable and stable reductions in clutter, difficulty discarding, acquiring, and functional impairment. CBT for HD includes efforts to boost motivation for behavioral change, training in effective and efficient decision-making, strategies to manage intense emotions, and cognitive strategies designed to help people look at their situation from a different, more adaptive angle.

So what do we know about the efficacy of CBT for HD? Studies show that the large majority of people receiving this treatment show a demonstrable improvement in their hoarding symptoms. Their homes are less cluttered, and their quality of life is better. So that's good news. The not-so-good news is that even after treatment, most people receiving CBT still have HD. That is, their condition is better but not gone. Ongoing maintenance is likely necessary. What that means to the fields of psychology and psychiatry is that we need to keep innovating. New ideas are coming up all over the place, from technical assistance to self-help to virtual reality to pharmacotherapy. Whether these novel innovations add to treatment outcomes remains to be seen.

You're holding one such innovation in your hands right now. The book you're about to read reflects a specific variant of CBT called *acceptance and commitment therapy* (ACT). In this book, you'll learn about changing behavior, thinking, and emotion through a dual process of accepting internal events, committing to meaningful behavioral change, and emphasizing behavior that reflects your values. Krafft and colleagues have synthesized years of research on this topic into a user-friendly guide that will help you move toward your goals.

So what's ACT all about? Krafft and colleagues are going to walk you through everything you need to know, but in brief, ACT is very much about accepting that you can't control your internal experiences—not very well, at least. But some people get so hung up on trying to control that internal experience—they try so hard to "fix" their feelings or make negative thoughts go away—that they lose sight of their values. Instead of living those values, they are focused inward, trying to achieve some desired internal state. ACT, then, fundamentally coaches you to redirect your efforts away from trying to feel or think a certain way, and toward behaviors that are consistent with your goals and values.

Here's a concrete example: Imagine that having to make decisions about whether to keep or discard things is emotionally taxing. Imagine further that you have a goal of getting your house cleaned. So you have a choice here: you can obey your feelings (that is, stay far away from what upsets you), or you can acknowledge that you feel upset and engage in behaviors that are consistent with your goals, nevertheless. In short, ACT is about putting your efforts toward living better, not just feeling better.

Overcoming HD is hard. I know this from years of research and clinical practice, as well as from hosting a TV series on the topic for many years. And I don't just mean physically hard—surely it is that, given all the possessions that need to be hauled and moved—I mean it's also emotionally hard. Letting go of attachments to objects, changing your perspective, and facing your fears are all very difficult things to do. But they're important, and this book is designed to help you along the way. I wish you the best of success as you move toward a life beyond hoarding.

—David F. Tolin, PhD

SECTION 1

Understanding Hoarding

CHAPTER 1

Introduction

We live in a time of unprecedented material abundance. To put it more simply, this is an age in which lots of stuff is available, much of it cheap or even free. Any person who lives in a modern society is confronted on a daily basis with decisions about stuff: what to get, what to do with it once you get it, and when and how to let go of things. Your kid brings home crafts from school a few times a week. You have to move to a smaller apartment after a break-up, and you don't have as much space to put things as you used to. You walk by the store and see there's a sale on dog toys.

For some people, those kinds of decisions are mundane, even mindless. They might get things they don't need once in a while, but they let go of many things automatically. They may do an occasional round of decluttering. The result is that their stuff and their space are fairly well-matched. They have more or less the right amount of stuff, and many of them don't even have to work too hard to keep it that way.

But for other people, managing the inflow and outflow of stuff is overwhelming, exhausting, or even excruciating. They might feel compelled to buy things they know they don't need, excited by the thrill of shopping or nervous about missing a good opportunity. They keep holding onto more stuff than easily fits in their home but find it difficult or painful to let go of most things. Many feel embarrassed by the state of their home and do their best not to think about their stuff at all. Some continuously work hard at letting things go, only to find that their space remains stubbornly packed with things.

If you're reading this book, we expect that you are one of those people—or perhaps someone you care about is. This book is geared toward people with what we call hoarding disorder. In this book, we're going to offer the best tools we know to help you develop a flexible, manageable relationship with your stuff, without treating your thoughts or feelings about your stuff as an enemy you have to defeat. If you are reading this because you love someone with hoarding problems, we hope this book will help you to better understand them and support them in addressing their hoarding problem.

What Is Hoarding?

If you wince when you hear the term "hoarding," you're not alone. Many people have images in their head of what "hoarding" is, often based on extreme cases or oversimplified stereotypes. Let's dive into what hoarding actually is.

Hoarding disorder is a psychological diagnosis defined in the *Diagnostic and Statistical Manual of Mental Disorders*. The DSM is essentially a catalog of different serious psychological conditions that affect people's mental health and behavior, defined by expert opinion and research. This means that hoarding disorder is a recognized psychological condition, like other diagnoses such as major depressive disorder, post-traumatic stress disorder (PTSD), or attention-deficit/hyperactivity disorder (ADHD). Hoarding disorder was first recognized as an official diagnosis in 2013, making it relatively new to the world of psychological research and treatment, even though compulsive hoarding behavior had been observed and described since at least the 1800s (Penzel 2014).

Hoarding disorder is defined by four criteria in combination. People with hoarding disorder experience the following: persistent difficulty discarding belongings, regardless of their value, because they feel like they need to save those items and would be distressed to part with them, which leads them to have clutter in active areas of their home that makes it difficult to use those areas in the usual way, and this pattern causes them serious distress or compromises their ability to do important things like maintain a social life, work, enjoy hobbies, or care for themselves. We can't diagnose anybody through a book—diagnosis requires working with a professional who gathers a lot of information to understand what's going on for a specific person. But in general, people with hoarding disorder hold onto so many things that their home becomes seriously cluttered in a way that causes problems in their life.

In some cases, you may have hoarding disorder without actually having a lot of clutter if someone else is cleaning up after you and clearing out significant amounts of your space. Also, people with hoarding disorder often actively acquire new belongings, but not always. Sometimes you can have clutter build up over time even if you do not buy or pick up many items, for example if you struggle to let go of everyday items like food containers and newspapers, or you inherit or are given large numbers of items.

You may notice that this diagnosis is in a sense unfair, or rather, reflects the unfairness of people's living situations. A person who can afford a three-bedroom house can fill up their garage and spare bedroom with stuff without it affecting their active living areas, while a person who shares a home with several roommates has to have very few belongings to keep their space clear. In addition, factors like being physically healthy and having leisure time can make it easier to declutter. But the core of the diagnosis has to do with how your belongings and your attachment to them impact your life—and this is usually what matters most to the people we work with.

Also, the distinction between someone having a diagnosis or not is arbitrary. There is no perfectly clear dividing line. If you feel that overall, you have persistent difficulties letting go of items because you feel emotionally attached to them, we expect that you may find this book useful whether or not you "officially" have hoarding disorder.

The Stigma Around Hoarding

Many people we interact with have a strong reaction to the term "hoarding." They laugh nervously and say, "I'm not like one of those hoarders on TV, though!" It's an understandable reaction. Hoarding disorder, like other psychological disorders, faces *stigma*—negative attitudes and behaviors directed toward people with this condition, including a sense of social disapproval (Bates et al. 2020). Discourse about hoarding in the general public and on social media often lacks nuance. Most people have had little opportunity to learn about the broad array of risk factors and life experiences that can lead to hoarding. Common stereotypes about hoarding oversimply a complex condition, which includes a wide range from mild to severe cases, and impacts people of all different backgrounds. Unfortunately, this makes it harder for people to seek help for hoarding problems.

In later chapters, we will talk about ways you can respond to stigma, to recognize it and acknowledge it without letting it control your behavior or define your sense of who you are. For now, we would just note that hoarding can present in many ways. Some people with hoarding disorder have only "clean clutter," in which you have large quantities of stuff but no health hazards like mold, pests, food waste, etc. Others do have unhygienic conditions in their homes. Some people with hoarding disorder hold onto items that other people would consider garbage, but many do not. Some people don't recognize the extent of their problem, but many do. In any case, respect and understanding, rather than confrontation, tend to facilitate greater insight. Moreover, the people with hoarding disorder that we've worked with are overwhelmingly a caring, thoughtful, passionate, hardworking, and creative group of people—the negative stereotypes about hoarding and our experience are different.

Other Causes of Clutter

Hoarding disorder isn't the only thing that can cause clutter. Clutter can be caused by changes in living situations, like having to downsize from a larger home to a smaller one. Hoarding behavior (such as saving lots of belongings) can also be caused by medical conditions like traumatic brain injury or a neurocognitive disorder like Alzheimer's (American Psychiatric Association, 2022). Clutter can also accumulate due to a different psychological condition. For example, a person experiencing a major depressive episode who has very little energy and a lot of difficulty starting any chores may have clutter build up in their home.

This book will be most relevant to those with hoarding disorder or similar problems. Hoarding disorder is not always, but most often a chronic condition in which clutter builds up gradually over time (Tolin et al. 2010). If there is another medical or psychological cause of hoarding, the onset of the problem is generally more sudden; however, there are exceptions to this rule. If you are wondering whether you or your loved one is experiencing hoarding disorder or there might be another physical or psychological cause of the clutter, we would strongly encourage you to talk with a doctor or licensed mental health professional.

How Do You Know If You Have a Hoarding Problem?

Hoarding can touch people's lives in many ways. If you feel seriously upset by the amount of belongings you have, or you feel driven to save your belongings, you might have a hoarding problem. People with hoarding may experience distress in different ways: for example, feeling overwhelmed, stressed out, or embarrassed by the amount of stuff in one's home, feeling extreme anxiety or anger when prompted to discard something, or feeling intense grief or fear when letting things go. Overwhelming emotional experiences are one signal of a hoarding problem. Another important angle is to consider how your saving habits, or your clutter, impact your life.

Think about different areas of your life as you answer these questions. Which of these apply to you?

- ☐ Does the amount of stuff you have, or your attachment to it, impact your relationships with friends or family?
- ☐ Do you find yourself frequently arguing with loved ones about how much stuff you have?
- ☐ Do you find it difficult or embarrassing to invite people over?
- ☐ Does your stuff impact your ability to care for yourself or look after your health?
- ☐ Does your stuff make walking around your home less safe or present a potential fire hazard by blocking exits?
- ☐ Does your home have bug infestations or moldy food around?
- ☐ Does your home have human or animal waste in places it doesn't belong?
- ☐ Does clutter in your kitchen make it difficult for you to cook meals?
- ☐ Does clutter cause you to neglect home repairs because you don't want to let others in or areas of your home are inaccessible?
- ☐ Does your clutter impact your leisure activities, making it difficult to engage in hobbies you used to enjoy?

- ☐ Does your stuff make it difficult for you to work?
- ☐ Is it hard to find important documents in your home due to cluttered spaces?
- ☐ Does clutter on your bed make it difficult to get a good night's sleep?
- ☐ Does clutter in your car (if you have one) make it difficult to offer others rides, to access parts of your car, or to see through all your windows?
- ☐ Does clutter affect any other important parts of your life?

If your clutter annoys you but does not interfere with any important areas of your life, you are less likely to have hoarding disorder. If your clutter, or your difficulty letting go of belongings, impacts any important part of your life like your family life, social life, leisure, work, health, self-care, volunteer work, etc., then this is a sign of a hoarding problem.

Sometimes these impacts may be obvious—having moldy food in your sink or fridge is obviously a risk for your health. But sometimes they are more subtle. Maybe your children have stopped wanting to spend holidays with you, and you're not sure if your clutter is part of it. Or maybe your clutter keeps you from doing repairs to your home, which could hurt your financial well-being in the long term. While it may be uncomfortable to consider, think about the full range of ways that hoarding may affect your life. Recognizing how clutter impacts you is a major step toward addressing hoarding.

Later in this book, we'll talk in depth about *values*—how you want to act and what you want to stand for in the world. Perhaps the most important question you can ask yourself is, does your clutter get in the way of living a meaningful life, of acting in ways that are consistent with your personal values? When you think about the kind of person you really want to be, does your stuff help you get closer to being that person—or does it take you further away from it?

One of our clients realized hoarding was impacting her values because she wanted to take better care of her health but could no longer find space in her home to practice yoga. Another client really valued being a welcoming and caring friend, and it pained him that he felt he couldn't invite friends over because he was ashamed of the state of his house. It is also worth considering how your stuff relates to your time. All of us have a finite amount of time available to us. The entirety of our lives consists of how we spend our time each day. Does managing your stuff take up too much of your time? Sometimes people with hoarding disorder routinely spend huge amounts of time sorting through their belongings, only to find that the amount they have hardly budges. Does caring for your stuff take up too much of your precious, finite time?

What Is the Goal of This Book?

We are four clinical psychologists with expertise in treating hoarding. We have all done a substantial amount of research to understand why hoarding happens and how to best treat it. Through our research, we've developed a way to treat hoarding using acceptance and commitment therapy (or ACT).

ACT is a form of psychotherapy that is based around a theory that normal human language and thinking processes can lead to immense psychological suffering. Specifically, our thinking patterns can trap us in rigid, unhelpful habits and lead us into fruitless, exhausting struggles to control our emotional experience, avoid unpleasant emotions, and cling to positive ones. ACT works by helping you to notice your thinking processes without being controlled by them, to step out of the battle to get control over your emotions, and to reorient your life toward pursuing meaning and purpose.

ACT has been studied in over 1,200 randomized controlled trials (the most rigorous way to test whether a treatment works; *Association for Contextual Behavioral Science* 2025). It is useful for not just psychological disorders like depression and obsessive-compulsive disorder

(OCD), but a broad range of challenges such as caregiver stress and burnout. The ACT approach we describe throughout this book is tailored to the unique experiences of people with hoarding problems.

We have conducted research on in-person psychotherapy (Ong et al. 2021) and online self-help programs (Krafft et al. 2023) to test our ACT approach for hoarding, and found that both types of ACT helped people reduce their hoarding symptoms and improve their well-being. In addition to our research background, we have used ACT with hundreds of clients, with all sorts of different problems, and we use ACT in our own lives. We believe that this approach in which we focus on identifying what truly matters to you, while bringing your mind into the present moment as it really is, recognizing limiting self-stories for what they are, and allowing your emotions to come and go as they will is genuinely liberating. It takes work, but the work pays off.

Our goal is to help you live a life that is more consistent with your values. If this book helps you to figure out what you care about and start to move toward it, we consider that a success, no matter how much or how little stuff you let go of. Whatever is most important to you—whether that's being a caring parent, a diligent volunteer in your community, or a creative and spontaneous artist—we want to help you make changes to your belongings and habits that help you engage in those important things.

Decluttering is a long-term process, and even if you are a dedicated reader and work hard to apply this book, you are unlikely to get to the very end of your decluttering journey in the near future—rather, think of this book as the start of a new chapter of your life. What do you want your new chapter to be about? Our goal is for you to make clear and meaningful progress in the right direction, following a path that feels sustainable, realistic, and worthwhile over time.

This book starts with information to help understand hoarding and what keeps people stuck in terms of hoarding habits in chapters 1 and 2. Then, in chapters 3 and 4, we focus on helping you identify what would make decluttering meaningful and make a realistic plan for decluttering. Chapters 5 through 8 focus on specific ACT skills that will help you to address common barriers to decluttering and sustain change over time, including skills for disentangling from rigid and unhelpful beliefs, developing the willingness to experience a broad range of emotions, decluttering and organizing effectively, and cultivating a flexible sense of who you are outside of your belongings. In chapter 9, we invite you to consider your values more broadly and in particular, how hoarding can impact your relationships and how to cultivate compassion and communication in your relationships. Finally, in chapter 10, we talk about how to cultivate meaningful action over time, and how to recommit when you drift away from acting in line with your values.

We encourage you to read this book at a slow and steady pace and give yourself time to practice the skills we describe before moving on to the next chapter. It probably won't be helpful to just read this book. Trying out the exercises and ideas within, and applying them directly to your own clutter problem, is crucial. We'd suggest reading one chapter each week, or whatever pace works for you to digest the material and put it into practice.

Who Is This Book For?

This book is mainly written for people with hoarding disorder or similar hoarding problems. We will use language like "your clutter" or "your problem" throughout, walk you through information about hoarding, and guide you to learn and apply skills that can help you disentangle from hoarding and live a life more aligned with your values. If you're a person with a hoarding problem, consider if self-help is a good approach for you. If your problem with hoarding is severely impacting your day-to-day life, you know you'll likely struggle to implement changes on your own, or you have other serious mental health challenges, we would encourage you to seek professional help.

The form of psychotherapy for hoarding with the most research support is called cognitive-behavioral therapy (Rodgers et al. 2021), and it focuses on changing your thought patterns and practicing discarding and not acquiring so that it becomes less upsetting over time. There are several other forms of therapy that have good initial evidence suggesting they work, including ACT, cognitive rehabilitation and exposure/sorting therapy (CREST) for older adults (Ayers et al. 2018), and compassion-focused therapy (CFT; Chou et al. 2020).

If you are seeking psychotherapy, we would suggest looking in the provider registries run by the International OCD Foundation or Association of Behavioral and Cognitive Therapies for a provider near you and asking if they offer any of those treatments. You can use this book alongside professional support too; we just encourage you to discuss this with your provider so you are on the same page.

Also, while there are no recommended medications for hoarding disorder, it may be useful to consult with a psychiatrist in your area in case you can benefit from medication. Some regions also have hoarding task forces, which vary in terms of what they involve but may provide or help coordinate resources like support groups, counseling, cleanup help, housing services, or services for older adults. There are other good self-help books available too. In particular, we recommend Tolin and colleagues' *Buried in Treasures*, a book that uses a cognitive-behavioral therapy approach and, like this one, is well-grounded in psychological science.

What this book—the one in your hands or on your device—offers that is different from other options is a way of working on hoarding that focuses on developing a compassionate, curious stance toward your thoughts and emotions, connecting with what you want to stand for in your life, cultivating the ability to mindfully observe your thoughts about your belongings and yourself, and implementing effective plans for decluttering rooted in an open, accepting, and aware posture. This ACT approach to working on hoarding involves a distinctive process of reorienting your life away from controlling your thoughts and emotions, and toward pursuing your values.

If you're a person with a hoarding problem checking out this book, consider whether this is the right book at the right time for you. One of the incredible aspects of people with hoarding disorder is their ability to see potential in anything. Our clients often have stacks upon stacks of self-help books and see each one as possibly holding the key to self-improvement. At the same time, many of those books gather dust.

Buying this book is not likely to help you very much if for whatever reason it becomes one book among a stack of books. You are likely to benefit only based on how much you mull over the book and actively apply it to your life. So, ask yourself (and respond honestly)—how interested am I in this book right now? How much time do I have to read it and apply the things I learn from it? Realistically, how likely am I to make use of this book? If this isn't the right time, you can always pick this book up at another date.

This book also offers insights for family members or caregivers on hoarding. You might have picked up this book not thinking about yourself, but because someone you care about has a hoarding problem and you want to know what to do. First off, we want to acknowledge that seeing someone you care about struggle with hoarding can evoke a range of emotions and is a very challenging position to be in.

We encourage you to read the whole book and use it to better understand the experience of your loved one with hoarding. Chapter 2, on the causes of hoarding, chapter 7, on the practicalities of decluttering, and chapter 9, which discusses how hoarding impacts relationships, may be particularly useful. We have additional free online resources geared toward family members or others who care about someone with a hoarding problem that you can access at New Harbinger's website. These resources can help you understand how to offer help and support effectively.

We also hope that treatment providers can use this book to learn more about how the ACT model applies to hoarding and how to tailor ACT to be most useful to people with hoarding disorder. We encourage providers to make use of the exercises and pointers throughout the book.

What's Next?

In the next chapter, we're going to describe our understanding of what causes hoarding based on scientific research. In particular, we'll talk about your mind, and why having a smart, creative human mind is a big part of your hoarding problem.

CHAPTER 2

Why People End Up Hoarding

We humans really like to have a clear story to make sense of our experiences. We are drawn to coherence—where everything makes sense—and to a compelling narrative. When we struggle, we seek answers. Even in a horrible situation—say a natural disaster or a terrorist event—one of our first priorities is to understand what happened. We want to develop a narrative about good people and bad people, fault and blame, causes and consequences.

Some of you may have thought a lot about what caused your hoarding problems. For example, we worked with one client who related her hoarding back to her abusive parents throwing out things she cared about as a child, and felt she was still rebelling against them. Other clients have had stories like, "I've always been a packrat" or "Everything was fine until I inherited so much from my parents." There is a kind of satisfaction in having a coherent story that explains how you ended up with a home full of stuff, even if you aren't happy about the situation.

In this chapter, we're going to walk you through what we know about the causes of hoarding in general based on research and experience. You may see bits of your story reflected here, others may not apply to you, and perhaps you'll notice some part of your experience that hasn't made it into your usual stories about yourself. To give fair warning, the story that psychologists can offer about hoarding disorder is not totally satisfying. We know much less about hoarding than we would like to know. Hoarding was only recognized as a unique disorder in 2013 (Albert et al. 2015). Because of that, hoarding research is still in its infancy compared to many other conditions. In addition, we know there isn't just one story of hoarding disorder—different people develop it through different pathways. However, we do know much more about what causes hoarding than we did ten or twenty years ago, and we also know quite a bit about how to effectively treat hoarding.

Behavior Patterns in Hoarding

Hoarding is by no means rare. Our best estimate is that hoarding disorder affects about 2.5 percent of people (Postlethwaite et al. 2019), which means that 2 or 3 of every 100 people has hoarding disorder. Even more struggle with clutter to a lesser degree. Hoarding disorder also gets more common as people age, so about 4 percent of people in their sixties have hoarding disorder, and about 6 percent of people over 70 have hoarding disorder (Cath et al. 2017). If those numbers don't seem large, keep in mind that hoarding disorder is more common than conditions like obsessive-compulsive disorder (Fawcett et al. 2020) or generalized anxiety disorder (Ruscio et al. 2017). Hoarding "feels" less common in part because stigma often drives people to keep their condition secret, and because it has not received as much attention within the mental health world as it should.

There are three big patterns that we tend to see when we work with people who hoard. First, your belongings may bring you joy, comfort, or a sense of security. The world of stuff may also feel like a door to endless possibilities. One of us was recently reading *The Outermost House*, a memoir about living on a Cape Cod beach, and ran across this beautiful passage: "All kinds of things 'come ashore' on these vast sands, and even the most valueless have an air of being treasure trove. The mysterious something moving from the swells into the breakers may be nothing but a smelly bait tub washed overboard from some Gloucester fisherman, or a lobster pot, or a packing case stenciled with a liner's name; but in the sea or on the beach a mile ahead it is something for nothing, it is the unknown, it is hope springing eternal in the human breast" (Beston 2003, 36). For people who hoard, items are much more than their physical or practical characteristics. They are hope itself.

Another major pattern is when it is really painful to discard belongings. If it feels excruciating to let go of things, you may find yourself keeping it all to evade those feelings. Doing so works to keep you from feeling that emotion, in that moment; but if you are reading this, you know that it takes its toll in other ways. This pattern is often closely tied to thought patterns we'll discuss in more depth later, like feeling that your items represent who you are, that letting them go would be a betrayal of the item or yourself or the person who gave it to you, or that discarding it would mean some kind of profound, personal failure. Everyone who has hoarding disorder experiences at least some of this emotional discomfort around discarding, but the intensity of it varies.

The third major pattern has to do with your attention and organization. Some people really struggle with the focus, planning, and decision-making involved in decluttering. They start by planning to work on the kitchen, and then they see a card that their friend wrote and five minutes later they've forgotten they were even trying to declutter. Decluttering requires a lot of skills: prioritizing, planning, getting the supplies you need, figuring out how much time it'll take to work on something, focusing on one area at a time, and deciding not just whether to let go of an item but how and when. If you find yourself feeling indecisive and confused, or just can't seem to make headway even when you are totally willing to declutter and are actively working on decluttering, you're not alone.

■ Case Story: *Nicole**

In this book, we're going to share a few case stories, and we'll refer back to them at times throughout the book. Nicole was in her early forties when we started working with her and completely overwhelmed by her life and her clutter. She had separated from her husband two years ago and had to move from a large house to a two-bedroom apartment, where she lived with her two young children. The apartment was stuffed to the brim, and Nicole was paying for two storage units she had filled during the move that she dreaded having to face and sort through. Nicole had always loved shopping and thrifting. She got huge thrills from finding good deals and unique items, and she loved to find items that reminded her of her loved ones and that she thought would make great gifts for them. However, since going through the separation and the stress of single parenting, she had fallen into a depression and was struggling with fatigue, exhaustion, and feeling unmotivated. Although she was struggling financially, she had trouble stopping herself from buying herself and her kids "treats" like makeup or new clothes. Looking around her space and seeing how even her kids' bedroom was full of boxes and bags, she knew she needed to declutter, but felt overwhelmed and ashamed at the prospect. In particular, she found herself ruminating on how upsetting it was to have to downsize and to no longer have a house for her kids, and how life had turned out so differently from what she expected. She desperately wanted to declutter so that her family could have enough space and so that she didn't have to feel ashamed and secretive anymore.

In later chapters, we'll talk more about how she worked to overcome her hoarding.

* Because we know hoarding is such a sensitive topic, none of these case stories is based on any one person—but they are realistic depictions that are based on the many different people with hoarding we've gotten to work with.

As we've mentioned, there are many factors that can play a role in hoarding. In the rest of this section, we'll discuss some of the more common ones.

Underlying Causes of Hoarding

Virtually no mental health condition has a single identified cause, and hoarding is no exception. Experts believe that, like other psychological disorders, hoarding behavior is caused by a complex interaction of genetic and biological factors, experiences of stress and adversity, patterns of beliefs and emotions, and your experiences with your belongings (Tolin 2023). If you have a hoarding problem, see if any of these causes might fit with your experience. If you're reading this book because you want to help a loved one who has a hoarding problem, ponder what some of the things might be that led them to hoarding. Your loved one is not a puzzle to be put together or a problem to be solved (notice that's the pull for coherence our clever minds go for), but getting curious about their experience may help you to build a better relationship with them and to support them effectively in decluttering.

Biological Factors

We know that hoarding runs in families, and about 36 to 50 percent of the risk for hoarding appears to be due to genetics (Tolin 2023). Some initial studies have found associations between particular gene variants and hoarding symptoms, but these genes are related to other mental health problems too and may not be predictive of hoarding in particular (Tolin 2023). Some studies have suggested that people with hoarding disorder experience relatively low activation of the brain and nervous system during decisions that are unemotional, but excessive activity when making decisions about belongings (Tolin 2023).

Stressful or Traumatic Experiences

Many people with hoarding disorder relate their hoarding behavior back to a stressful or traumatic life event (Landau et al. 2011), and hoarding is associated with traumatic events (Preworski et al. 2014), relationship upheaval and interpersonal violence (Tolin et al. 2010), and excessive physical punishment in childhood (Samuels et al. 2008). That said, not everyone with hoarding disorder has had these sorts of experiences. There is also some research suggesting that people with hoarding disorder may have difficulty forming close, trusting relationships with others, possibly because significant people in their lives were not warm and supportive, which leads them to rely on objects as a source of comfort more than other people do (Chia et al. 2021).

One thing this research suggests is that for some people, hoarding may have helped you during a vulnerable time in your life. If you have gone through really hard things like being raised by neglectful or abusive parents, or experiencing violence or trauma, hoarding may have helped you feel some solace or comfort. In some circumstances, hoarding may have been the best option available for you to cope with adversity, even if now, its costs outweigh its benefits. It might sound like an odd question for this book, but it's worth considering—has hoarding helped you? Do your belongings give you a sense of security, or control? Have they been a source of comfort when you were vulnerable, isolated, or had chaotic relationships? Did your hoarding come about after a traumatic or stressful experience?

Thought Patterns

One thing that certainly plays a role in hoarding is your thoughts. There are certain types of thought patterns we see over and over in people with hoarding disorder.

BELIEFS ABOUT OPPORTUNITY

You may see items as representing unique opportunities that would be upsetting to miss out on. You don't want to throw away a newspaper without looking through it, because there could be something important or fascinating to learn about inside. People with hoarding problems are very often curious, intelligent, and eager to learn everything they can. They might look at the books in a bookstore and feel like they need almost all of them. You might worry that if you let an item go, you're missing the opportunity it presents, or that you will miss it or need it if you give it away.

BELIEFS ABOUT RESPONSIBILITY AND MORALITY

People with hoarding often feel a profound, moral sense of responsibility for items. You might believe that you are morally obligated to care for your objects, to make sure they are used, or to make sure that if you discard them, you do it in the most appropriate way possible. This can veer into perfectionism, a sense that only the ideal way of letting an item go is allowed. For example, one client we worked with felt it wasn't good enough to just take her children's old toys to a thrift store when it was time to let them go. Instead, she felt she needed to find a person who had kids of the right age and whose kids would definitely enjoy playing with them. Similarly, if she had a kitchen appliance break down, she believed it was her responsibility to get it repaired, even if it would be costly to do so and she no longer used the item. She had held on to a broken blender and toaster in order to repair them, even though she hadn't been able to find anyone who could repair them, and she had bought new ones to use years ago. Although she really wanted to declutter, she struggled greatly with doing so because she felt such a high degree of responsibility to her items, and she defined that responsibility in specific ways.

Responsibility and perfectionism are also related to beliefs that it would be absolutely terrible to "make a mistake" by getting rid of something you later regretted or getting rid of something in the "wrong" way. Sometimes these beliefs are tied to commitments to environmentalism and the desire to make sure nothing goes to waste. There is nothing inherently bad about these beliefs—most items are resource-intensive to make, and the world as a whole would be better off if people wasted less. Yet, when these beliefs cause you to fill your home with things that you don't have space for, they have a large personal cost.

BELIEFS ABOUT MEMORY

Beliefs about belongings and memory often come up as well. You might worry that if you don't keep an item, you won't remember something important, like a task associated with it. You fear that if you recycle the business card that a heating company gave you, you'll forget that your air conditioner is supposed to be cleaned. People with hoarding disorder often feel that they not only need to keep reminders but to leave them in a place they'll see the reminder, or otherwise they'll forget about something important. It may also feel important to save something because you want to hold onto a specific memory. Perhaps you keep your mother's silver because you strongly associate it with your warm memories of your mom preparing a holiday dinner—and you worry you might lose those memories if you gave it away. People with hoarding often report feeling like they have poor memory and attention, even though rigorous research has not found consistent, objective evidence of problems in memory or attention among people with hoarding disorder (Stumpf et al. 2023; Zakrzewski et al. 2022).

BELIEFS ABOUT IDENTITY

Sometimes, your belongings also feel as if they define who you are—that your whole identity is wrapped up in the things you have, and if you did not have them anymore, you would lose your identity. We've worked with clients who feel like if they give away things from when their children were young, they lose the sense of themselves as a parent. We've also worked with clients who feel like if they threw out half-done repair projects, they would be turning their back on being a handy and capable person. In what ways are your belongings tied up with your identity?

OTHER COMMON BELIEFS

Sometimes, people who hoard think of objects almost like other people that they have a relationship with; in that case, giving away an item can feel like an act of betrayal or personal disrespect. Another important thought pattern—and this is a bit nuanced—has to do with your beliefs about your ability to tolerate challenges or unpleasant emotions. It can be profoundly hard to get organized while having beliefs that you can't tolerate feeling upset or embarrassed. If you believe you can't handle feeling upset or anxious, you're more likely to ignore the problem or put off dealing with it.

Some thought patterns that occur in hoarding have to do with other people. You may worry that if other people touch your things, or move or organize your things, they'll lose them or do the wrong thing with them. Those beliefs may be based on lived experiences in which others were inconsiderate. Not everyone with hoarding feels this way, but some people feel a strong need to control their belongings.

EMOTIONAL REACTIONS

Just like this vast spectrum of thoughts, people with hoarding experience a range of emotions related to acquiring things, saving things, organizing, etc. You may feel fear or worry about the prospect of letting items go or not having something you need. You might also feel sadness, grief, dread, or frustration when you face your belongings. For example, getting organized might involve looking through the belongings of a spouse or parent who passed away, or might put you face-to-face with how bad the condition of your home has gotten over time. Sometimes you might actually feel quite angry about some of the things in their home—for instance, if a parent keeps giving you things you don't want but feel responsible for, or if some of the clutter was caused by another member of your household.

Many people, once they have committed to working on their belongings and get started, actually feel mainly positive emotions about discarding, like enthusiasm. One study found that when people with hoarding disorder were prompted to discard items, while many felt anxiety, fear, or anger, many others felt joy or surprise (Dozier 2019).

For many, hoarding is also tied into emotions of embarrassment and shame. Shame is a complicated emotion, and if you're anything like us, a deeply painful one. Shame is a form of distress that is tied into a sense that you've done something wrong—you acted out of line with your expectations for yourself, or someone else's expectations for you. Some experts have claimed shame is fundamentally bad, and while we can understand where they're coming from (feeling shame really hurts), we believe that shame serves a purpose just as each of our other emotions do.

Humans evolved as social creatures who were reliant on being part of a group for our very survival. Experiencing shame when we violated a taboo or broke a rule may have kept our ancestors alive in tough circumstances. In our modern lives, shame can be a powerful message and motivator. It can help us realize when we're doing something wrong, and prompt us to try and make it right. When you lose your temper and raise your voice at your spouse, feeling ashamed of your behavior can motivate you to apologize and to commit yourself to being more patient in the future. Shame is much more likely to lead to positive behavior change when we can see a way to repair the problem, and we believe that our attempt to repair it is likely to be accepted by others.

Shame can also lead us to try and hide, withdraw, and not face any more scrutiny than we have to. Almost everyone we've encountered with a hoarding problem has felt some degree of embarrassment or shame about their living situation. At times, it motivated them to try and address it, but more often, it led them to hide their problem from others as best they could, and sometimes to try and ignore it entirely. It is also fair to question whether shame is merited.

Because shame is so closely linked to social norms and expectations, we sometimes experience shame in ways that are unfair or we don't rationally agree with. In eras when some groups treated disabilities as shameful, people with disabilities probably experienced shame; that shame was unfair and unhelpful. As we've mentioned, hoarding is a stigmatized condition, and we believe it should be understood as a mental health condition like any other. If you experience shame, we'll talk more in the future about responding to that shame in ways that work for you, whatever caused it. We will also share quite a lot in upcoming chapters about ways to navigate your emotions without either rejecting them or letting them control you. For now, see if you can recognize, and acknowledge, the emotions you experience related to your hoarding problem as well as where they might be coming from.

Other Mental Health Struggles

Hoarding disorder can occur all on its own, or it can be related to other psychological conditions. Among people with hoarding disorder, depressive disorders and anxiety disorders are common. About half of people with hoarding disorder also have major depressive disorder, which involves feeling very sad, low, or numb, losing interest in activities, and disruptions to sleep, appetite, and energy (Frost et al. 2015). About half of people with hoarding disorder also have an anxiety disorder such as generalized anxiety disorder, which involves persistent, uncontrollable worry, or social anxiety disorder, which involves extreme fear of being viewed negatively by others in social situations (Frost et al. 2015). About 28 percent of people with hoarding disorder have inattentive ADHD, which involves being easily distracted, trouble organizing tasks and staying on task, and forgetfulness

(Frost et al. 2015). About 18 percent of people with hoarding disorder also have OCD (Frost et al. 2015), which involves recurrent upsetting and unwanted thoughts and/or repetitive behavioral rituals that you feel compelled to do.

In broad strokes, depression may lead to hoarding or make hoarding worse by sapping your energy, making it extremely difficult to motivate yourself and to start on tasks, making it harder to make decisions, and depriving you of positive emotions or beliefs. People with anxiety disorders and OCD may be particularly likely to worry about the consequences of discarding the wrong things, not having things they need, or losing information. ADHD can make it challenging to tackle clutter because it is harder for people with ADHD to plan out and prepare for a complex task like decluttering, even to get started and to remain focused while organizing.

Case story: *Marco*

Marco was in his fifties when we met him. He was married with one adult son who had moved out a few years earlier. He had never been diagnosed with ADHD but strongly suspected that he had it. He described himself as someone whose mind never seemed to stay on one task, who had always had trouble sitting still and who always seemed to be brimming with ideas and projects. Marco had taken up many different hobbies over the years, from model trains to rock collecting to genealogy, and when he got engrossed in a hobby, he ended up purchasing or collecting all sorts of tools and supplies for that hobby. However, it didn't always keep his interest over time, and rooms in his home were often full of haphazard piles of supplies and kits, as well as projects he'd started and not finished. He had trouble letting any of those items go because he really intended to come back to the hobbies or projects and felt that all those items were still useful.

His wife Anita was also a "packrat," and while she didn't bring in as much stuff, she had trouble letting go of any items from their son's childhood and also had large stashes of books and yarn that she wasn't willing to downsize. While Marco and Anita had a strong relationship, they both thought the other person was the main "clutterbug" and the one who needed to declutter.

Additionally, Marco and Anita were passionate environmentalists and hated the idea of letting anything go to waste. They held onto clothes, craft supplies, food containers, leftover wood or supplies from any home projects, and anything else that they thought might still have a use. Marco had every intention to work on decluttering but always seemed to end up focusing on something more fun or interesting like a new hobby or upcoming trip. However, after decades of increasing clutter, Marco was tired of having so much stuff around. He didn't want to be like his father, who lived in a hoarded home until he passed away. He wanted to make enough space that his son would come visit again.

Perfectionism and Procrastination

There are other psychological factors at play too. Many people with hoarding disorder have difficulty making decisions and find themselves going through mental loop-de-loops. Some people have a tendency toward perfectionism; they hold themselves to high standards and are upset when they can't meet all of their expectations for themselves. They have trouble giving themselves credit for the progress they make or making their standards flexible enough to move forward.

Most people with hoarding problems also get stuck in procrastination. They have lots of ideas and plans for cleaning out their home, but life gets in the way, it doesn't feel like the right time, or they just have trouble getting started on it. Procrastination is more or less a universal experience; every one of us authors has put off doing something important we needed to do because we didn't feel like it or felt intimidated to start it.

Procrastination feels good in the short term; it's a relief to decide you're going to wait to tackle that one really bad closet until you're up to the task. Unfortunately, those important-but-hard things often don't get easier over time, and sometimes they become even harder. In a very real sense, the only time that matters is this moment, right now, because the current moment is the only one you can take action in.

Case Story: *Judith*

Judith was in her late sixties when we worked with her. She lived in a small home out in the countryside. She grew up in a household that looked perfect from the outside, but where she was abused and berated by her father any time he perceived that she had made a mistake, broken a rule (no matter how small), or not achieved something he expected of her in academics or sports. Judith held herself to high standards and, even as an adult, felt terrified at the prospect of making any mistakes or not living up to her obligations. As a child, her stuffed animals and dolls had provided immense comfort within a home that was unpredictable and terrifying, and she felt deeply attached to them and protective of them. Throughout her life, she kept letters, cards, mementos, artwork, and books she had read, and she felt a strong sense of caring and responsibility toward each item. She hated the idea of missing any important information or regretting discarding anything, and she found parting with items to be anxiety-provoking at best and devastating at worst.

Although her home was always cluttered, the amount of stuff really got out of hand when her parents died and she inherited their things. Although their furniture and boxes of their belongings took up so much space they made her living and dining room unusable, she felt completely stuck. She knew that looking through her parents' belongings would bring up both terrible feelings of loss and awful memories of being terrorized by her father, and she couldn't figure out what the "right" thing to do with their belongings would be. Judith's wife was initially patient with her hoarding tendencies but had become increasingly frustrated and critical as months and then years passed after inheriting Judith's parents' belongings without progress. Judith was driven to seek treatment because she was worried about the strain on her marriage and was feeling increasingly desperate to declutter.

Hoarding Is Not Just an Individual Problem

We've been talking a lot about your thoughts, emotions, and behavior, but hoarding is not just about an individual—it takes place in a broader world. In addition to the kinds of traumatic experiences we talked about earlier, your relationships can have profound connections to hoarding. If you were raised by parents who hoarded, it may have made you associate home with clutter or made it hard to learn how to keep tidy.

If you live with someone else who has a lot of things, whether they have a hoarding problem or not, that can make it complicated to declutter. You don't just have to confront your stuff but disentangle it from theirs—and it can be disheartening if they aren't motivated or willing to get organized when you are.

Feeling rejected or criticized by family for your stuff can also be profoundly upsetting and disheartening. We've known clients who took a huge step toward decreasing clutter—say, recycling a stack of old catalogs—only to hear family members say things like "Great, now just do the other twenty piles and we'll be getting somewhere." If you're reading this book because of concern for a loved one, we strongly encourage you to watch out for falling into this trap, and to appreciate even small steps in the right direction.

Also, many of our clients are lonely, an experience that is all too common for people with hoarding disorder (Yap et al. 2023). Loneliness might make you more likely to turn to your objects for comfort, or make you feel indifferent to your clutter. To all of you who are reading this, we hope you have supportive people in your life who want the best for you and gently encourage you—if not right now, then someday.

The Abundance of Stuff

Zooming out even further, hoarding also has to do with our social world. We touched on the abundance of stuff today in chapter 1. One study of people with garages in Sacramento found that more people use their garages exclusively for storage than exclusively to park their cars (Volker and Thigpen 2022). Throughout the majority of human history, it would have been rare if not impossible for the typical person to accumulate large amounts of stuff. Today, it is commonplace in many countries.

This isn't necessarily a bad thing—it's in fact pretty wonderful that most people in high-income countries can usually afford the basics of life like clothes, furniture, and food. But it does mean that we are living in a time when there is a quantity of stuff available like never before. While research on this topic has been pretty mixed (Fontenelle et al. 2021; Landau et al. 2011; Walji & Salkovskis 2024), some people who hoard believe their attachment to their things, or attraction to new things, has to do with experiences of deprivation or poverty in their past, or a family member's past.

Stigma and Stereotypes

Finally, stigma toward hoarding disorder ironically feeds into hoarding. We can divide hoarding stigma into two major features: public stigma (negative and rejecting attitudes among the general population toward hoarding) and internalized stigma (negative and rejecting attitudes toward hoarding among people who have hoarding disorder). Public stigma can be linked to discrimination, in which people with hoarding are treated unfairly. Public stigma can also lead to internalized stigma over time as you are exposed to negative beliefs about people who hoard and your mind applies them to you (Vogel et al. 2013).

One study of hoarding stigma broke it down into three components: difference (perceiving that people with hoarding are unlike others), disdain (perceiving people with hoarding as bad or unworthy), and blame (perceiving people with hoarding as at fault for their condition; Chasson et al. 2018). We hope the information we've given so far makes it clear that hoarding is a mental health condition like any other, with a complex series of causes. It can be treated and people can recover from hoarding, yet that doesn't mean you are to blame for having it. Stigma can make people feel ashamed and hopeless. Among people who have significant hoarding symptoms, stigma is a barrier to seeking help (Chasson et al. 2018). The stress associated with stigma or discrimination can also feed back into hoarding problems.

You didn't choose for hoarding to be stigmatized, and uprooting stigma (whether public or internalized) is not an easy task. But we do believe there are ways to respond to it as effectively as you can. We also think that it's the role of everyone, including family members, mental health providers, and everyone else, to challenge narrow stereotypes about hoarding and create a more nuanced and empathetic understanding of this complex experience. In our work, we strive to communicate accurate information about hoarding and to relay realistic and relatable stories about people with hoarding problems. As someone with hoarding, choosing to share your experience with others, even one trusted friend, can be a powerful way to destigmatize hoarding and communicate how hoarding impacts real people. At the same time, hoarding stigma is real and you are the only person who can choose whether or not disclosing your hoarding to others makes sense for you and is consistent with how you want to act in the world.

Our recent research demonstrated that the ability to put yourself in someone's shoes is closely related to hoarding stigma (Krafft et al., under review). Whether you are someone with hoarding, a family member, or a treatment provider, we strongly encourage you to try imagining life from the perspective of the people with hoarding that we mention in this book. It may help you be more empathetic toward yourself and others and disentangle from hoarding stigma.

The Power of Your Mind

Perhaps you've already read a bunch on hoarding, and much of the above is familiar. What we have to offer is a way of understanding how people get stuck and stay stuck in hoarding problems, and how to get unstuck. This theory can be summed up in one sentence: you developed a hoarding problem because you have a top-notch human mind. Maybe that sounds facetious, like a cruel joke, but it isn't.

Humans are, as far as we can tell, unique creatures because our minds are constantly not just learning new things but actively forming associations and rules that completely change how we act. You know how people used to talk about cyborgs—a human that is so enhanced by machinery and robotics that it's almost a new species? Well, modern humans are essentially mind-borgs—our mental machinery is so powerful that it transformed us as a species, and the world along with us.

Let's make this clearer. People learn some things through direct experience. Picture being a young kid and eating carrot puree for the first time—if it tastes good, you eat more of the orange goo. If it tastes bad, you spit it right back out. But as we learn to understand words, develop language skills, and relate things in our minds, less and less of our learning comes from direct experience. If I offered to make you some butter mochi, and told you it's a sweet and chewy Hawaiian dessert made with butter, sugar, and rice flour, you might very well decide that you want to try some (or not) even if you've never once encountered butter mochi before, based on the associations you have with the concepts of sweet, dessert, chewy, butter, and so on.

These human minds, which allow us to learn things without direct experience, are absolute marvels. They've helped us with huge advances in technology and science. They also help keep us safe. If you're a parent, it's a huge relief once your kid understands things like,

"Don't touch that plant, it'll hurt your hand" without needing to first get injured from touching the plant. It's a gift to learn some things through language rather than direct experience.

But these exact same thinking abilities have a dark side. If you learn that alligators are dangerous, and that the local nature preserve has alligators, you might stay away from it—even if you may never see an alligator there, and being in a beautiful natural place would bring you joy. Our minds can tell us to be afraid of things we've never experienced, can predict bad things in the future, and can compare ourselves to other people or to our own ideals and tell us we don't measure up. When it comes to hoarding, your mind can tell you that buying that new shirt will change your life, and suddenly you'll feel like a competent professional on the inside. Your mind can tell you that you can't handle letting go of your grandmother's art. Your mind can worry about what will happen if you let things go, berate you for wasting anything, and tell you it is your job to make sure every item finds a perfect use.

Our minds have the power to separate us from, and distort, our direct experience of life. If you ever try to paint realistic pictures, you will quickly discover that while your mind says with certainty "the sky is blue," it's often completely wrong. When you truly pay attention to what you see with your eyes, the sky may actually be purple, grey, brown, white, or all sorts of combinations of those colors.

How does this play out in hoarding? Well, your mind may be full of rules and expectations and obligations that make you feel compelled to get or keep things. Your self-judgments and standards feel pressing, real, and urgent, and it's hard to recognize that they are the work of your mind. If your mind says, *Someone could use those yogurt cups*, you automatically keep those yogurt cups. You might feel like there's a tug-of-war in your mind whenever you start to think about sorting or discarding things (*You have to let some stuff go! But you can't just get rid of it: be responsible!*) and you can't move forward until you win the tug-of war.

In this book, we will teach you the best ways we know to step out of the tug-of-war entirely, and to loosen up the grip your mind has on you. Our beliefs about ourselves can be especially old, rigid, and constraining. Whether your mind says you are "responsible" or "caring," "lazy" or "pathetic," your mind probably has some well-worn stories about who you are and what it has to do with your things. Connecting with a part of yourself that is bigger than any of these stories and has the capability to step back and observe them can help you have more freedom.

Sometimes our minds pull us out of the moment we're actually in. Our attention gets taken over by worries or fantasies about the future or by reminiscing or thinking back over the past. When that happens, we can miss what's really going on right in front of our noses. You might fantasize about saving your daughter's toys and giving them to her kids someday, and miss paying attention to your actual interactions with her. You might think about all the lovely things you could do with a new sewing kit, but never actually sit down to sew in *this* moment.

All the planning and forecasting and remembering abilities we have also lead us to fall into two traps we mentioned before: avoidance and attachment. Your mind can make you more fearful that you might regret letting an item go, can make you feel grief as you associate a belonging with a certain memory or time in your life, or can make you feel you have a relationship with an item almost as if it were a person. You mind might also tell you that it's bad or wrong or reflects poorly on you if you feel fear or grief, that you can't handle being upset, or that it's essential for you to feel good all the time. Your mind may make it much harder to let things go, while at the same time convincing you that changing those habits would be too hard or impossible.

Many people who hoard feel that they are pushed around by their thoughts or feelings. For example, Marco, the environmentalist client we mentioned before, felt extremely guilty throwing out plastic containers that weren't recyclable. For years, he diligently washed and kept the containers that came into his home. While he found uses for a small number of them, they kept piling up and taking up more space on his shelves and floor. He felt like he just couldn't face the guilt of letting them go, even though he had no use for them and hadn't been able to think of someone who would. His mind said he had to find a use for the containers, and that it would be too wasteful and harmful to throw them out. Keeping the containers worked to placate his mind—but it did so at the cost of taking up too much of his space, which ultimately made it hard to use his pantry and kitchen.

What do you do to placate your mind? Do you feel trapped by the need to placate your mind? Do you long for a life that is less focused on pleasing your mind and staying comfortable? What might be possible if you didn't have to do what your mind said?

What's Next?

In chapter 3, we will ask you to explore this question in depth. But we encourage you to take a pause and start to mull it over. If you didn't have to do as your mind said, if you didn't have to follow its rules—what would you want? What would you long for? What would you want more of in your life?

SECTION 2

Skills for Addressing Hoarding

CHAPTER 3

Finding Motivation Based in Meaning

Motivation is simultaneously simple and incredibly complex. On one level, motivation is *anything* that influences your actions. We're motivated to eat by hunger—or by seeing that shiny pastry in the bakery window. We're motivated to rest by fatigue. We're motivated to work because we need money to live. We're motivated to care for the people we love. All of our actions are motivated in some way—some by needs or reasons so basic we barely notice them.

Motivation is also fickle and fiddly. We talk about needing to "get motivated" or "find motivation." We think and talk about motivation as if it were equivalent to energy, enthusiasm, and positive feelings. We grab after motivation, and it slips through our fingers like sand. We have the best reasons in the world, the most important possible motivation to change our behavior—like quitting smoking so we can have more years with our loved ones—and yet we still struggle to keep that motivation in focus, to *stay* motivated.

What Motivates You

If you picked up this book, we can safely guess you *are* motivated to get organized and make more space in your home. That is, there is something about decluttering that is important to you. Sometimes you may feel more motivated than at other times, but there is something, some set of reasons and influences, making you care about the possibilities decluttering might hold for you. If you're similar to people we've worked with, what motivates you likely falls into a few different categories.

Placating Others

First off, you might want to declutter to appease other people in your life. Maybe there's someone in your life who keeps asking you to clear more space, who gets annoyed or embarrassed by clutter in your home, or who worries about your safety. You might not agree with them completely, but their opinions might be one factor pushing you to declutter. You might feel criticized, belittled, and misunderstood by family and friends. It might feel like decluttering is the key to get them off your back. Like Judith, who was worried that her marriage would crumble if she didn't address her hoarding, many of our clients are motivated to declutter because they know others want them to.

Controlling Your Emotions

You might also be motivated to declutter by negative emotions. You might feel embarrassed by the state of your home. Sometimes, you might feel overwhelmed and exhausted when you look around and *really* notice all the things you have. Sometimes, people with hoarding feel ashamed—that they can't believe their problem has become so serious. You might find that you start trying to declutter and get organized when you are most frustrated with yourself. In this case, decluttering is motivated by something you don't want to feel anymore. On the flipside, you might also motivate yourself with the desire to feel good, maybe even fantasizing about how relaxed or proud you'll feel once you get your back bedroom cleared out.

Changing How You Feel About Yourself

For some people, decluttering can be motivated by wanting to think or feel differently about yourself. We know lots of people with hoarding problems who are organized and efficient in their careers, and desperately want to feel as capable and on-the-ball when it comes to their homes. If you are self-critical, or have a tendency toward perfectionism, it might feel like getting your clutter under control would ease your self-judgments or harsh inner voice.

Avoiding Problems

Sometimes, people want to declutter to avoid negative consequences. These can range from minor concerns, like not wanting to accidentally let food expire because you couldn't spot it behind everything else in your pantry, to major concerns, like fear of being evicted from an apartment. If you're someone who feels compelled to buy things, you might want to avoid draining your bank account further or having to declare bankruptcy. If the consequence is serious and imminent, it might be a very strong motivator, at least temporarily.

Improving Your Life

You may also want to declutter because you want to experience positive consequences, because you see some possibility within decluttering that would make your life better. This might include improving your relationships with important people in your life, making it easier to have friends over or engage in activities you like, and making it easier to take care of yourself. You might dream of the day when you can surface all your art supplies and sit down and begin the paintings you've wanted to work on for years.

EXERCISE: Notice What Motivates You

Take a moment to consider what usually motivates you. It may fit into the previous categories, or it might be something else. Which factors make you feel most motivated to declutter? Which factors lead to you actually working on getting organized or letting things go? Which ones do you intentionally think about, which ones do you experience but try not to think about, and which ones just aren't relevant for you? We encourage you to take a few minutes and write about this in a journal, notepad, or note-taking app, but you can also ponder it internally.

Now, take a moment to consider how stable that motivation is. When you're motivated by self-criticism, or the desire to get your kids off your back, or wanting to get your finances in order, or whatever tends to motivate you—how strong is that motivation, and how long does it last? How consistent is it over time?

Some Kinds of Motivation Are Fickle

What our experience, and a substantial amount of research, shows is that some kinds of motivation tend to work better than others in the long term. Or in other words, relying on certain kinds of motivation is like trying to build a house on top of sand. Decluttering is hard work, and to make progress requires patient, persistent effort—it needs a solid foundation.

If you're decluttering to please other people, that motivation is likely to come and go depending on how those other people are acting. If you're decluttering to ease your self-judgments, you may find that your inner critic bounces back pretty quickly even when you make progress. In *The Spirituality of Imperfection: Storytelling and the Search for Meaning* by Ernest Kurtz and Katherine Ketcham (1993), the authors write that "To teeter at the extremes of self-love and self-loathing, to pursue perfection because we despise our imperfections, is to find neither satisfaction in successes nor wisdom in failures." Decluttering out of self-hatred or self-criticism is, in our experience, unlikely to better your life in any way.

In general, if you're motivated to declutter by trying to avoid something—to avoid a negative emotion like frustration or shame, or to avoid a negative consequence—your motivation is likely to be unstable, and your work on decluttering is likely to be less rewarding, less creative, and less flexible than it could be.

As a thought experiment, if there's something you find quite frightening, think of how you act when you're around it. For example, if you're seriously afraid of snakes, and you see a snake, your attention and action all narrow in on that snake, and getting away from it as quickly as possible. Avoiding something can be very motivating, but its effects are brief and it narrows how we act to a small window of possibility. Decluttering because you're fed up with yourself might work when you're feeling that frustration intensely, but it won't keep you coming back to declutter once the next day rolls around.

Alternatively, picture a situation where you're motivated by positive consequences—for example, interacting with an animal you like. If you like rabbits, and you have a chance to interact with one, you might hold it, pet it, play with it, give it snacks, or watch it run around. Your behavior is broad, flexible, and more likely to continue. We think focusing on positive consequences of decluttering is particularly important and likely to give you the strongest foundation for decluttering. Yet, one type of positive consequence is especially important—acting in ways that are consistent with your values.

What Values Are

The term "values" can mean different things. To us, values are ways of acting that are inherently meaningful to you and can help guide your actions. You might value being an affectionate spouse, or confronting challenges head-on, or being a patient caregiver, or being attentive and curious and learning more about the world. The potential values people might find most deeply important are infinite. When you know what you care about most, and when you know you are taking steps in line with what you care about most, there is something deeply fulfilling in that alignment—something likely to help sustain you through the hard work of decluttering, to dignify that work. In fact, our previous research shows that disconnection from values is linked to worse hoarding symptoms and lower life satisfaction (Ong et al. 2018).

Up close, people's values vary as much as their fingerprints do, but when we zoom out a bit, there are broad qualities of values that give them their potency. Values have a positive quality—they reflect something you want more of, something to strive toward, something you want to increase or expand on in your life. This aspect is critical for helping you be consistent and flexible in pursuing your goals. Something like "I want to stop disappointing my kids" or "I want to stop having to worry about my things" is not likely to serve as a helpful value because it focuses on avoiding something negative. It is more powerful to go toward something you care about.

Values are also broad and flexible—there are many paths toward a value, and its meaning isn't likely to run out anytime soon. Being an affectionate spouse could be served by making space for your husband's clothes in the closet, or by bringing him an iced coffee, or by sharing a funny story. The actions involved in being an affectionate spouse might change a lot as your circumstances change—say your husband is deployed and your chances to interact are much more limited—but there are still paths available, even if they look quite different.

A related point is that values are something you can enact in your own behavior. No matter how important something is to you, if it's something you have minimal control over (like being loved by others, or having the respect of your community), it's unlikely to be helpful as a value. On the flipside, you might find a value within it, if there is a part of that goal that is fundamentally meaningful and that you can connect to your actions.

Another key point is that values provide *intrinsic* motivation. That is, it is inherently meaningful to pursue a value, whatever the outcome. If you value being a caring parent, you might choose to keep asking your surly teenager about their day even if you know they'll probably brush you off. If you value taking on challenges, it could be rewarding to confront your clutter head-on even if you don't see progress as quickly as you would like. Similarly, your values are *yours*. They might be informed by other people in your life, but values are most helpful when you choose them based on what you genuinely care about, rather than pleasing other people or doing what they expect of you.

What Values Are Not

These unique qualities mean that values are, so to speak, their own beast. They are distinct from goals that you have, from the ways that you feel, and from the things that you own.

Goals are defined by a specific outcome, and once you finish your goal, you're done with it. Values are broader than any one goal. Values are the bigger picture that can make our goals meaningful. Goals are basically like a to-do list: you write down your to-do list, then when you're done, you cross the goals off and toss out the list. Values are a bit more like a personal journal—you keep writing and reflecting over time, and you're never "done" with a personal journal, because you can always write more. Your values can be useful for setting goals (in fact, our next chapter is on connecting values to goals), but values go beyond any specific goal. Wanting to clear out your storage unit is a goal; wanting to savor your hobbies is a value (which could be served by clearing out your storage unit).

Values are not the same as our emotions, and values don't always "feel good." Because values are defined by meaningful ways of acting, our values and our feelings aren't always the same. For example, if one values being a kind parent, they might choose to play or talk in a caring way with their kids, even when feeling quite frustrated with them. Or if one values persistence, they might carry on organizing books for twenty minutes a day even when they feel tired or disinterested.

To put it another way, values make it *worthwhile* to do something, even when it's hard or we aren't feeling the way we'd prefer to. In fact, getting in touch with our values can be painful. As Dr. Kelly Wilson, one of the developers of ACT, says, "Values and vulnerabilities are poured from the same vessel." When you really consider how much you value being a kind parent, memories of all the times you were impatient or harsh with your kid might pop into your head. When you engage with the values that make you want to declutter, you may feel shame, frustration, fear, or fatigue. Values reflect what matters to us so much that it is worth making room for pain and difficulty to pursue them.

Now let's dig into the ways that your values, and your belongings, are related. If you let yourself imagine your deepest values, the things you truly want to stand for in life, the patterns of action that would constitute using your limited time on earth well—your belongings and what you do with them probably aren't the most important part of your life. You probably wouldn't want your tombstone to say either "She had a lot of space in her house" or "They had every item they needed." Yet, here you are working on building a different relationship with your belongings. So, there's something meaningful about that.

How Decluttering Might Serve You

You are the only person who can say why decluttering would be meaningful to you specifically, but we'll share a few observations from working with people who hoard. Some values have relatively clear connections to decluttering. There are two broad categories we see a lot of—values related to relationships, and values related to things that would be easier to do when you have more space.

First off, you may feel that decluttering would help you be the kind of parent, partner, roommate, or family member that you want to be—that decluttering could be an act of care and kindness toward the most important people in your life. This is different from decluttering to please others in subtle but important ways—it focuses on your actions (rather than their reactions) and on the positive (decluttering as an act of caring) rather than the negative (getting people off your back).

For example, when we first started working with Judith (chapter 2), she knew her clutter was taking a toll on her marriage, and she knew she "should" declutter, but she couldn't get herself started. Identifying her values around decluttering was eye-opening. She talked about how she really wanted to be present and attentive to her wife, and to do little things to make her smile like bringing her coffee in bed, or sitting with her to eat a nice meal at their dinner table, and she noticed how clearing space in her home would make it possible to live out her values.

Other times, there may be activities that you want to do that are connected to deeply held values that would be well served by making more space or organizing your belongings in ways that make them easier to use. People with hoarding problems often have many craft supplies, or tools, or a pantry packed with interesting herbs and spices, but don't have the organization or space to actually use those items in the ways they would like. For example, our client Marco wanted to get back to building model train sets, but he usually couldn't find the tools or items he wanted within his clutter, and he didn't really have enough space to sit and work on those projects. If there are activities that you think would be enabled by decluttering, consider what is meaningful about them—creativity? Challenge? Growth? Commitment? Play?

Some of your values may be connected to decluttering in ways that are more tenuous, but still important. Maybe you value acting in ways that will improve your health, and having your home be more organized would give you more mental bandwidth to focus on building a new exercise habit. Maybe (even if you have many years ahead of you) decluttering feels like a gift you could give your children, so that they don't have to make decisions about your belongings in the future. Can you imagine any ways in which decluttering might facilitate other values—even the ones that aren't directly about your space?

Another way to think about your values and your belongings is to consider qualities of action you want to bring to working on decluttering. You're reading this book because you want to address clutter, saving, or acquiring in your life. But you could do that in all sorts of different ways—you could do it harshly or gently, you could do it inattentively or diligently. You might want to bring qualities like curiosity, flexibility, persistence, or independence to decluttering. Are there ways of acting that you want to embrace, that would be meaningful in how you approach working on your things?

EXERCISE: How Are Your Values Related to Decluttering?

Take a moment to consider this: what are some of your most important values, and which ones would be served by decluttering, getting organized, or having more space? If you're willing, we'd encourage you to write down a few notes about five to ten values that are especially important to you, that stand out as qualities you'd like to embody. You could write these on a journal or notepad, or in a digital document.

When Your Values Support Holding Onto Things

You might be starting to think "Hey, you're stacking the deck here! You're only asking about values that would be served by letting go of things—what if my values tell me to hold onto things?" If so, you're not wrong! First off, it's worth pausing to consider if the reasons you hold onto things are truly about your values—the positive attributes you want to strive toward—or about avoiding something upsetting, like the fear of making a mistake or doing something wrong. That said, sometimes people's values do play a role in holding onto things. We've worked with many clients who care deeply about being of service to others and hold onto things for that purpose. Many people with hoarding problems genuinely care about protecting the environment and reducing waste.

When you notice that one of your values might be served by keeping things, we would gently encourage you to ask a few questions: First, is pursuing this value in this way effective? Will saving my old containers prevent waste and reduce landfills? Second, are there other ways that you could pursue this value? For example, if you care about being of service to others, brainstorm a few ways other than holding onto things that you could pursue this value: you could also help someone by mowing their lawn, or bringing them a meal, or listening to them attentively. You may find that some of your values are well served by keeping things—and that's an important thing to notice if so—we'd just encourage you to stay open to other possibilities too.

Identifying Your Values

Even if you already have some thoughts about what your values are, it's worth spending some time exploring them. Your values are the foundation for the rest of the skills and goals we'll walk you through in this book. Values are the base we'll build from, the compass to tell you which directions to move in, and the cairns that tell you if you're on the right path. There are a lot of different ways to help identify and clarify the values that matter most and will serve you best.

One way is to think about the different areas of your life. Some areas of life that your values may connect to include family, work, marriage or intimate relationships, friendship, recreation/fun/leisure, education/learning, community, spirituality/religion, physical health, mental health, parenting, and caregiving. Are there any areas that stand out as especially important to you? Within those areas, how do you want to act? What kind of parent, friend, or worker do you want to be? How do you want to care for your physical health, or spend your leisure time? Usually, our clients are quick to identify values that involve being useful or kind toward others. But also ponder, how do you want to act toward yourself? Would it be meaningful to you to be kind or patient with yourself? To challenge yourself? To care for yourself flexibly, or compassionately? If you're reading this book because you have a loved one with hoarding disorder, think about your values for interacting with them. What qualities do you want to bring to that relationship?

Another approach to identifying your values that can be powerful is to think about the people you admire. Who is someone that you look up to, that you think deserves respect and admiration? What qualities do they bring to their actions? For example, let's take Dolly Parton (a beloved figure if there ever was one). If she's someone you admire, you might be impressed by her generosity, her creativity, her humility, her entrepreneurship, or her sense of humor. (Did you know she once entered a Dolly Parton drag queen contest, and lost?) If you think about the last thing you read, or watched, or a game you played, or an image you saw that really moved you, sometimes you can find a value lurking inside that emotional reaction, too.

Your imagination can also help you to identify some very real values. For example, close your eyes for a few minutes and picture how you would like your life to be different in a few years. What would your home look like? What would you be doing differently? How would you be spending your time? Imagining how you'd like things to be different can be uncomfortable, as you might find your mind generating all the reasons things can't be different, but try to focus on what those images say about your values. If you picture yourself sitting on the couch reading, but you never do that now, is there some deeper value connected to reading? What would it mean to you?

One classic way to identify values is to imagine what you would want written on your tombstone. For example, would you want your tombstone to say, "Here lies Jamie, she was a caring and welcoming friend" or "Here lies Jamie, she was a creative and diligent artist"? While it might sound a bit morbid to think about, values are intimately connected to the reality that all of us have limited time in our lives. The poet Mary Oliver famously asked, "What is it you plan to do with your one wild and precious life?" If you were told you had a year to live, you might make some dramatic changes to take the trips you've always wanted to take, to spend more time with loved ones, to finish a project that's important to you.

Yet, while all of our lives are finite, we rarely live day-to-day with a sense of *urgency* to spend our time on what matters most. Many of us feel a large gap between what is most important to us and how we spend our time. We're aware that in the big picture, we'd like to be using our time differently, but the demands of the day take over, and the hours and days are gobbled up by the least meaningful things possible—checking emails, doing paperwork, sitting in traffic. Your specific circumstances may make it especially difficult for you, for example if you are struggling financially, working long hours, or living with a serious health condition.

Yet, if you want to spend your time in ways that matter, the only option is to identify what matters with you and begin to take steps in that direction. In our experience, it's an option that pays off—even if at first, you can only move a tiny bit closer toward being the kind of person you want to be. One question you might ask yourself is this: What are ways I could spend my time today that would be a gift to myself?

Connecting With Your Values

Hopefully, the previous section has helped you to consider and identify some values that are genuinely meaningful for you, and that can help guide you in considering how and why you want to declutter. Knowing your values is an important step. But in the same way that knowing *how* to ride a bike and being *able* to ride a bike are two different things, knowing what our values are is not quite enough to make and keep us motivated. It is, in fact, alarmingly easy to lose sight of your values when life gets hectic, or you're feeling down, or just as time passes. Connecting with your values is a process in itself. There are many ways you might do this—here are a few ideas.

First off, it can be helpful to set an intention focused on your values. For example, before you start organizing a certain part of your house, you might choose a particular value that this is related to, or a value that you want to embody, like "I'm going to work on organizing my art supplies while bringing forgiveness and understanding to myself for having so much." Writing it down or saying it out loud can be especially helpful. You might set an intention at the start of the day, or for a shorter period like the next fifteen minutes. While all your values may be deeply important to you, we'd suggest focusing on one at a time so you can give them the attention and commitment needed to connect with them.

Having reminders of your values can also help you connect with them regularly. For example, if you use a paper calendar, you might try writing one value that you want to focus on at the start of each week. Sometimes our clients have found it helpful to write an especially important value on a sticky note, and stick it to their car dashboard, or bathroom mirror, where they will see it regularly (although if you already use a lot of visual reminders like this, keep in mind it may be hard for a new one to stand out). Writing in a journal about your values, at the end of the day, or at a certain time of the week, can help keep them fresh in your mind. If it's possible, it can be quite helpful to block out a time in your calendar—even fifteen minutes a week—to check in with yourself about how things went in pursuing your values in the last week, and what value you want to focus on for the next week.

Finally, when you are doing something aligned with your values, try savoring the experience as if you were savoring a delicious meal, noticing and appreciating each detail. If you cleared a space to do yoga in your home, slow down and notice all the sensations that go along with doing yoga. Savor the feeling of being able to move your body in your home. When you're bringing bags to the donation center, even if it brings up mixed emotions, see if you can savor a sense of progress, and appreciate the ways in which you are serving your values.

If you're similar to the clients we work with, you might be gearing up to try every strategy we just mentioned to identify and connect with your values. But we'd suggest focusing on one step at a time. Develop a rough, initial list of your values, and try one of the strategies for connecting with them in the moment. Give that strategy a little time, and then check back and see how it's working for you, and if you want to try a new one. Keep in mind as well that your values may change over time, or you may discover new values along the way. Some of your values may "work" better for you than others, and it may be helpful to focus on those.

What's Next?

Your values for decluttering can help you get motivated more consistently to declutter, but they need to be translated into effective, useful patterns of action in order for you to make the progress you would like. As such, our next chapter focuses on developing specific plans for action based on your values.

CHAPTER 4

Forging a Path Forward

In acceptance and commitment therapy (ACT), there is a strong focus on values. Again, values are the things in your life that are meaningful enough to you that you would put your time and energy into them, and not just because they are fun. Values usually match something that we care about at a deeper level. Values are generally unachievable; they are more like a direction we might set for ourselves to head in (say, heading east).

Connecting Goals to Values

The neat thing about connecting our day-to-day behavior to our values is that it can guide us in each step of our lives. If someone has a value around parenting, they can make choices in each moment to be the best parent they can be. They will pretty much go their whole lives without ever accomplishing being a wonderful parent, and that is okay. We are not supposed to be able to accomplish our values, just like we will never arrive at "east." But being able to connect to that value is still excellent because it can guide us in each little step.

Before we move on to setting goals around decluttering, make sure you know why it's important in terms of your values. What values would reducing the number of items in your house serve? Another way of saying it is, what would be meaningful about decreasing clutter for you based on the things you care about? The same would apply to bringing things into the home. What values would you be supporting by bringing fewer items into the home? Making a plan to declutter and putting it into place involves focus and hard work. What values would dignify that work?

SMART Goals

SMART goals are a common acronym for ways that we can create behavior changes in our lives. These goals are common in business and educational settings. SMART stands for specific, measurable, achievable, relevant, and time-based. We will go over each one of these concepts in the following paragraphs, but let us just take a second to capture why it's important to choose goals that are going to work for us.

Sometimes the clients we work with get fed up with their clutter. They want it dealt with *now*. They don't want to live like this anymore. This happened with Nicole in chapter 2, who had downsized to an apartment. She asked her mother to watch her kids for the weekend and planned to get her apartment organized. She was fed up with the piles of clothes in her home and how hard it was for her kids to find space to sit and draw. She grabbed some boxes and started putting in anything she thought she could let go of. As she wandered around looking for things she could discard, she felt overwhelmed at the task.

Even after filling up a box with odds and ends, she could see little improvement. She found her mind going on a loop, wondering how she had let things get so bad. She also realized that she couldn't make much of a dent without working on her clothes, but she realized she didn't have time to photograph and list all the clothes online to sell in one weekend. After a few hours, she was exhausted and dispirited. She had filled up a few boxes with items, but she wasn't sure what to do with them next and she felt more overwhelmed by her apartment than ever.

After we started working with Nicole, we encouraged her to break down decluttering into a series of small steps that would move her in the right direction, like sorting through one kitchen cabinet each day, or photographing and listing five items to sell. Once she had planned and selected a small, achievable task, she had much more success with following through. Completing the goal she set helped her stay motivated and feel a sense of accomplishment. Some days, she didn't meet her goal and was frustrated, but other days, she would set a goal to go through one drawer and then end up doing two or three. As she stuck to setting achievable goals, she started to see the impact in her home.

Let's move on to breaking down SMART goals.

Specific. If you were going to give your child a curfew, you wouldn't say "I'd like you a home bit earlier tonight." You're going to have more success saying, "Please be home at 10:30 tonight." The same concept applies to our work with saving and discarding. Instead of saying "I'm going to decrease the clutter on this table," find a more specific action. More specific goals could be choosing an amount of time you might do the work, choosing a number of things you'll throw away, or looking at a particular area and saying, "I'm going to clean off this square." Hopefully doing the work this way keeps it from being so overwhelming.

Measurable. You'll notice all the goals that we just wrote were measurable. All three of the examples given were quite clear. If you stated it to another person, they could come in and judge whether or not you completed it. We want you to do the same thing with your goals. State them in such a way that you have 100 percent certainty as to when you finish the activity. This will also help you know how much time you must commit to this activity.

This is important because without making your goals specific and measurable, your brain will start to trick you in the middle of activity. It'll tell you, "You've done enough. That's a lot for you. Are you sure you made the right choice?" We want to take that struggle off the table. Approaching it this way takes a lot of the guesswork and pressure out of the activity.

Achievable. We assume by now you know that we believe our minds don't always tell us the truth about our current situations. Our minds can blow things up and make things seem a lot bigger and more difficult than they really are. While you're reading this book, it's very possible that you could make a reasonable goal to work on in the next couple days. But what we predict will happen is, when you step away from this book, and are put in a real-life situation, your mind will find that goal to be overwhelming. Some people can power through it and still accomplish the thing they need, but there are a lot of people who, when put in an overwhelming position, feel stuck and won't move forward.

We would rather that you choose a goal that is ridiculously easy so that even if you are in a tough situation there is an incredibly high chance you will do it. We would rather you do something small, and feel like it was too easy, than plan for something big and then do nothing. It's well known within our field that as you start taking small steps forward, slightly larger steps will feel easier. When you make a goal in this area, make it so small and straightforward that there is a 90 percent chance it'll happen. If you're reading this book because of a loved one with hoarding, this is especially important. You need to set goals (or offer help) based on what's achievable for your loved one, not what you could do in their shoes. That might look like helping them fill up one bag to donate to a food pantry or offering to help them sort through clothes for fifteen minutes before dinner.

You might say, "I need to make bigger goals; I need to take care of this problem." Anyone who's ever invested money, paid off a big bill, or worked toward a large goal, knows that many small steps strung together can result in something big. We like to think of it like a graph, and as long as you are moving a half a percent or 1 percent toward your value, you will eventually start to get really close. There are 365 days in a year, and if you just move a quarter percent forward every day, you will quickly be there.

Relevant. A goal is made relevant by seeing how it fits into the bigger picture. If you're a basketball player shooting free throws in practice, one throw doesn't "matter," but as part of a bigger aspiration to train for success, each one can have meaning. You can make them feel relevant by treating each one as though it's training for an important moment in an important game. We want you to interact with your goals in the same way.

As we listed before, saying "I'm going to spend fifteen minutes discarding" is specific, measurable, and achievable. But we can amplify this by asking ourselves how those fifteen minutes of discarding will move you toward things you care about. Will this give you more opportunities to cook a home-cooked meal? Will this make you more likely to invite someone over? Will this give you a sense of accomplishment, and is that worthwhile to you? Like the basketball player shooting a free throw who's thinking "if I can get better at this now, I'll be able to make the shot when my team needs me to," you can focus on the "why" of the behavior change you have committed to.

You might be thinking, "well, of course everything I'm doing around my hoarding is important." And while that's true, it's easy to be disconnected from that importance *in the moment*. But you can develop the skill of treating each bit of decluttering you do as though this is an important moment and there is meaning behind it. Picture each bit of time you put in like a piece of a large puzzle, and think about what completing that puzzle will mean to you and do for you.

Time-based. Self-control is a fascinating thing. You probably exercise self-control in lots of ways. You might prep for a work project or study for a test in advance, work hard now so you can get a promotion or better job, eat well and exercise to stay healthy in the long term, or be saving money for retirement or a later larger purchase. All these things involve giving up something now for something bigger later.

The SMART goals are another example of that. We are choosing to give up a little enjoyment right now and instead do something difficult, with the understanding that we will reap the benefits in the future. But it doesn't mean it's easy. When tasked with the question of, "should you fill a garbage bag with trash, feel all the discomfort that comes with that, carry that bag out to the trash, and then sit there with your distress for the next couple hours," many of us would choose to just watch a television show. One of the ways to increase the likelihood of doing a difficult task now is to shrink the timeline.

Instead of thinking that you need to eventually clean out this house, stop bringing stuff in, or do better with your clutter, it probably works better to go at it with the plan of "I have to get one garbage bag of trash out of this house by Thursday." That SMART goal is more within your abilities and hopefully less overwhelming.

We have an expression in therapy called *the power of the appointment*. You can probably guess what that means. It means that a portion of the behavior change we see in our clients is simply from them being aware they're going to come to a session, and we are going to ask about what they worked on over the week. The power of the appointment is simply a deadline for a behavior change. Knowing that someone's going to ask whether they did it or not is enough to make it happen.

We know this is the case because it is common that the clients did the work we planned the day before the session; heck, sometimes it's hours before the session. This is okay. One of the things we tell clients is, when our course of therapy ends, leave the appointment time in your calendar. In your mind, you can still harness the power of the appointment by just pretending that we are going to check up on you once a week. And what would you tell us? What were your gains over the last week?

Therefore, in this situation we want your goals to also have a reasonable time restriction. We want you to make a goal that you can accomplish and that also has a reasonable duration. Don't make the cutoff so soon that it's hard to fit in with your other life obligations, but also don't make it so far away that it really means you'll just sit there for six days and then do the cleaning. It's also reasonable to think that you only want to do this work every so often. You may have other things in your life that you're working on. We suggest making deadlines, perhaps somewhere in the range of every two days to two weeks, for your behavioral commitments that will work for you and keep you motivated. You can increase your sense of accountability by having a supportive person check in with you after your deadline and ask how it went.

EXERCISE: Select a SMART Goal and Commit

Write down one SMART goal that you are going to work on, starting within the next few days and continuing for at least a few weeks. Check to make sure your goal fits all of the characteristics: specific, measurable, achievable, relevant, and time-based. In the following bullets we offer general examples of behavioral commitments that are often helpful. You may choose whatever works for you, but it can be helpful to see some examples to get you in the right zone. Please be creative and adjust these to fit you. Then, commit to following your SMART goal. Writing about the values it is connected to may also be helpful. You can download a worksheet from the webpage for this book to write down and keep track of your SMART goals.

- Choose to remove a certain number of items each day.
- Limit the number of items that can come in each day.
- Choose an amount of time you will spend removing items each day.
- Choose a particular area you will clean out.
- If you have many of one type of item, decide how many you will keep and discard the rest by a specific date.
- Limit the amount of time you spend churning through your items.
- If you struggle with finding the right home for an item, make a commitment to throwing a set number of items in the trash or in recycling.

- If you have a large item like a dishwasher or a car, the commitment could be calling someone who can come look at it for removal.
    - A second commitment could be paying them to remove that item.
- Order a small dumpster.
- Invite a friend or a loved one over for a set amount of time of cleaning out.
- Commit to removal of "one box worth" of items.
- Commit to cleaning out a certain room or storage unit by a date.

What to Do When You Get Off Track

Some of you might be worrying about what happens if your progress stops or starts to go in the wrong direction. Let us calm that worry. You are going to mess up. You are going to get off track. We can think of very few instances in life where someone embarks on a huge project and consistently works on that project until it is completed.

We predict any number of things will get in your way as you work on your clutter. Some will be completely on you, others will be because of things out of your control, and many will be a mix. We hope that you just walk into this project with the goal to do your best and the awareness that some moments will go well, and some moments will not. We have never seen a graph of behavior change that is a straight line. They all have their ups and downs.

The key is to generally keep your graph going in the right direction. We are okay with days or weeks that don't go as well as others. We just don't want you to fall into a trap where you quit trying if something doesn't go well. The common traps people fall into are usually cognitive in nature. What we mean by that is your mind says something to you about your mistake, and you buy into that thought and change your behavior plans.

Let's pretend your plan is to spend ten minutes cleaning off the table every day for the next week. You accomplished this for three days and then hit a part of the table that was harder than you anticipated, and you get nothing completed for the next four days. Your mind says to you, *It looks like you're not ready to do this. Maybe this is too hard and you need to wait until you're feeling less stressed.* You might buy into that thought, doing what it tells you to do, and stop working. Instead, we would want you to notice that your mind will say things that are not helpful from time to time, recognize that your mind said those things, and still choose what you want to do. In that moment it is completely possible to choose to either work on that harder part of the table, or just choose to go in a different direction.

For example, if you choose to go in a different direction, you might leave the table as it is and make a new behavioral commitment to discard five newspapers a day for the next week. Yes, it's true that the table got the best of you. But like we said earlier, as long as your graph is going in the right direction, we think you're doing great. There's no speedometer on you. This is not a competition. If you are getting things out of your house regularly, you will make visible and meaningful progress.

After you work on the newspapers, maybe you will choose to work on some items you've been saving in the closet. Who knows, maybe after a couple weeks of success in other areas, when you make a commitment to work on the table, it will feel different. Maybe it will be easier. If not, that's fine; just make a commitment that there's a 90 percent chance you will do that is more within your ability at this time.

To sum this section up, it's better to think about your work with clutter like you might think about a relationship. We don't enter relationships with the expectation that we will always be perfect. Our expectation is that we will do our best, and sometimes we'll mess up, and when we mess up, we'll say we're sorry, and then continue to do our best. If we left a relationship whenever we made a mistake or said something hurtful we didn't mean, we'd all be pretty lonely. When we think about behavior change, your line will have ups and downs—that's the default.

Making Difficult Choices

Before going further, let's acknowledge that making choices can be difficult. Not just around discarding—even though this may be especially true—but even choices as seemingly mundane as what to eat for dinner or what show to watch after dinner. So, set the expectation that these decisions are going to be challenging. That way, you won't be caught off guard later. Then, let's also acknowledge that you've done many difficult things in your life—whether it's raising a child, losing someone you love, living with clutter, or even admitting to yourself that you need help.

Doing difficult things is not new to you, which means you can do more of them. At the same time, we don't believe in making things more difficult for ourselves than we need to. Let us provide some practical guidance on how to make choices around your belongings that are intended to make those difficult choices a little bit easier.

Seek Support from Others

First, if it's possible in your life, find a supportive person to help you. You don't have to go through this alone. Even if the person doesn't actively help with decision making, having their emotional support could make a world of difference. If you trust their judgment, you could ask them to weigh in on your decision making, especially where you suspect you lack perspective. This doesn't mean asking them to make choices *for* you—that would be depriving yourself of autonomy. Rather, it means allowing yourself to consider other opinions when making your decisions and widening your own perspective. Chapter 9 will talk in more detail about how to make asking for help as smooth and successful as possible.

Make a Plan

Second, make a medium- to long-term plan. When setting your SMART goals, consider how to put multiple goals together to make a longer-term plan that can be achieved through a series of SMART goals. Exactly what this medium- to long-term plan looks like depends on your needs and capabilities. For instance, if the area most impacting your well-being is the dining table surface, it might be worth starting there. If you know you're the kind of person who is good at leveraging momentum, choose a weekend to tackle the entire dining area and start with the easiest items to get rid of. But if you're the kind of person who feels easily overwhelmed, then take it slower. Perhaps set a goal to get rid of three items on your dining table a day. Regardless of what you decide, make sure the plan is something you can follow through on for at least one month. This means only biting off as much as you can chew.

Evaluate Your Items

Third, when it comes to actually choosing what to keep versus get rid of, rank your belongings in terms of how much you need them, even if it feels like you need everything, so you have a sense of *relative* importance. As you rank your belongings, consider what scope is feasible. For instance, choose a limited set of related items to start, such as your kitchen utensils or office stationery—as opposed to everything in your kitchen. If you can't see all your items at once, it's fine to estimate (e.g., making your best guess about whether something is in your top 25 percent of stationery items, your bottom 25 percent, or the middle).

Ask yourself how much you use—not how much you *plan* to use—each item. Is this item something you need to own or can you borrow it? For example, if you make margaritas once a year and have a generous neighbor who is willing to lend you their margarita machine whenever you want it, perhaps you can afford to donate yours. As you evaluate your need for each item, be honest with yourself. Remember what we said about expecting this process to be hard. If it was easy, you wouldn't be reading this book right now. We talk in more depth about strategies for evaluating items and choosing what to keep in chapter 7, so if you find yourself really struggling with how to evaluate your items, you may want to consult that chapter. Or if your mind starts throwing a million reasons at you for why you should keep each item, chapter 5 may be helpful. Decluttering is hard, and you can do hard things.

Sort Your Items

Fourth, physically organize your decisions. For each area or set of items you sort through, create two to four piles or boxes based on what you will do with the item (e.g., keep, donate, put in trash, give away, recycle, or sell). This will help you see the effects of your decision making more easily, such as whether you are keeping much more than you are getting rid of. Use the order of priority you established in the previous step to aid your decision making. Start with the items of least need, or items that you never use, and work your way up. We recommend putting most or all of the first few items in a "leave" pile, so you gain confidence in your ability to let go of things.

If you recruited someone to support you on this journey, this is where their gentle encouragement may be useful. Once you've made your piles, physically move them closer to where they're supposed to end up. For example, put your discard box next to your trash can, or put your donate pile in your car so you can drop them off next time you drive by a donation center.

Try It Out

Fifth, test out living with your decisions. If you're able to donate, sell, or discard the items in those boxes, ignore this step. But if you're struggling to fully let go of them, strike a compromise. Put those boxes out of sight or give them to someone to hold for you for at least two weeks. If you're feeling bold, you could even tell them to automatically get rid of those items if they don't hear from you in two weeks.

The goal here is to experience what life is like without those items in your life. How much are you bothered by losing these items versus helped by the space gained from getting rid of them? How much worse is your well-being without those items? If you don't notice a significant difference, perhaps you might not have needed those items as much as you had originally thought.

Organize Your Space

Finally, if you're at the point where you are organizing whatever items remain, consider what organization system will work best for you and those who live with you. For instance, if you live alone, you could mirror your physical organization with your mental organization that makes sense to you and no one else. But if you live with family, you probably want to consider a more generic organization system that makes at least some sense to everyone. Either way, consider how items are used in your home throughout the day. That will give you some idea of what things go together. Ultimately, there is no "correct" organization strategy. Good organization is whatever makes your life easier or improves your well-being in some way.

We will talk in more detail about organizing items in chapter 7, but if you need ideas for where to start, consider two common ways to organize: by function or use case, or by similarity. For function, you would group items that tend to serve a similar function, like putting everything you need for laundry (e.g., laundry basket, detergent, bleach, dryer sheets) or all your baking tools (e.g., baking trays, cookie cutters, spatula, stand mixer) together. Grouping things by function makes it easier for you to access everything you need for specific activities.

The other way of organizing by similarity means grouping things based on what category they belong to, so you could put all your kitchen appliances (e.g., stand mixer, blender, air fryer) or board games together. As we describe these options, you might notice one making more sense to you than the other—try out that strategy.

Once you clarify what kind of organization works best for your household, start there. That is, start from where you want to end up, so you have a plan for your items prior to physically organizing them. Coming up with categories while organizing makes it more likely that you'll be making decisions based on your items, rather than the lifestyle that will work for you. Make sure you have a vision for the set of items you're organizing at the outset. For the same reason, if possible, organizing by those final groups can be more helpful than organizing by location. For instance, rather than starting with your living room, then bedroom, if you have your crafting supplies scattered throughout your home and have them grouped together in your organization plan, then go ahead and grab those first. Let your plan be your guide.

What's Next?

We're guessing you have a lot of familiarity with your mind objecting when you start to declutter. So next up, we're going to talk about the role of your mind, and how to navigate it when your mind is full of roadblocks to decluttering.

A Brief Check-In

When you work on making changes and trying new things, it's a good practice to pause every once in a while to consider how things are working. At this point, you're several chapters into this book, and hopefully you've had a chance to try out some of the ideas and exercises. Take a moment right now to reflect on the following questions. If you like to write, you can write down your responses in a journal, but it's also fine to just ponder them:

1. What new things have you learned that have been especially helpful so far? These might be things you want to especially focus on continuing to practice, remember, share with loved ones, and otherwise work on.
2. What strategies haven't been helpful and why? We wrote this book hoping each of the skills might be of use, but everyone is different and some of these strategies might not be working the way they are intended. The important thing is to find ways to make changes in your life so you can meet your goals with working on your hoarding and in living your values more broadly. So if something isn't working, that's okay, and let's focus on finding what will help.
3. What progress have you made working on your hoarding? Even if it's small things, consider what changes you have made.
4. What do you want to keep working on?

We'll check in again after a few more chapters.

CHAPTER 5

Recognizing Your Mind at Work

In many ways, the function of a human mind is to help us live as safely and effectively as possible. The things that our minds do most naturally are look for dangers, plan ahead to not get ourselves into problematic situations, and predict future problems and think about ways to solve them. Basically, your mind is like a wonderful assistant. It watches over you, guides you to do the best thing you can, and looks for problems that might happen in the future and tries to protect you.

When it is working well, your mind is a huge asset. If you look at how humans generally live on the planet earth compared to every other living thing, our minds have been incredibly helpful. Our access to basic needs like food and shelter—as well as intangibles like education, art, and belonging—are all achievements that rest on what human minds can do. We would not trade with any other animal.

Minds Are Helpful and Unhelpful

Perhaps your mind is doing its job right now and saying, "What these authors are suggesting isn't totally true—I sure don't like how everyone's mind works and sometimes don't like my own." And we agree. Arguably humans have it the best on this planet and at the same time we may have it the worst. We judge and criticize ourselves. We have envy. Even when things are going great, they're not good enough. We have a hard time forgiving. You might have everything that you need, and your mind can still tell you that you need more or remind you that you could lose it all. Strangely, that same mind that tells you to pay your taxes, get your oil changed, or reminds you that a new show has come out and you probably should watch it, can also convince us to do things we regret.

Our minds are wonderful and a problem. Your mind likely plays a big role in your hoarding problem. Your mind might be making sure that you have everything you need, leery of any risk that could come from throwing out something important. Your mind may also be highly creative, attuned to any benefit that your belongings could provide to you. Your mind can convince you that you might miss something important if you recycle your mail without checking each page, or that a fancy new juicer will transform your health. Our minds are there for sensing danger, identifying problems, predicting, planning, and preparing, and they don't come with an off switch.

Reacting to Your Mind

The good news is we have an answer to this problem. Basically, your mind is like a smartphone that's constantly sending you notifications. Sometimes the notifications are helpful and sometimes they aren't. Luckily, you are a human being with free will and with practice you can choose when to listen to your mind and choose when not to. This might sound surprising or like an oversimplification (does your mind have a lot to say right now)?

But take a moment and reflect on your everyday experience—we would guess that there are many times when your mind tells you to do something, and you don't listen to it. Sometimes your mind says you should go to sleep, and you stay up anyway. Sometimes your mind tells you to go buy some candy, and you choose not to. Even when it comes to your things, we'd guess that once in a while your mind tells you to hold onto something, and you choose to discard it anyway. We believe you are quite good at ignoring your mind—and that you can get even better at it.

The mind can be tricky. It has ways of convincing you that unimportant things are really a big deal. Let us give you an example: say you are walking to work and you have the thought, "I wonder if it's time to water my ferns." Maybe that thought was prompted by seeing someone else out gardening, but it doesn't really matter because it's just one of many unimportant goofy thoughts that pop up throughout the day. You are not near your fern right now. You haven't seen it wilting or anything. This is sort of an unimportant thought for this moment in time, so you just let it go.

Here's another example. You look up at the sky and see a few dark clouds forming and you think, "I hope it doesn't rain today because I have my nice shoes on, and I don't want to get them wet." This thought is maybe a little bit more important and maybe you look at your phone to check the weather or maybe you look around you to see if there are more dark clouds. But you don't really buy into this thought too much and you keep walking to work.

Now let's take a decluttering example. You're walking to work and you pass by a nice stool that someone set next to their garbage can, and you think, "That is a beautiful stool that someone could use and if I don't do something about it, it is just going to end up in the dump." Now just like the other example, those words are just a thought in your head. You have a choice to respond to them or not.

Even as we type them, we can appreciate that those thoughts grab you in a different way from the previous examples. They have more power. They have more pressure. They're trying to protect you from something useful being wasted. You may not feel like you have a choice when they turn up. Your predicting and planning mind is thinking about the ways that that stool could be used. Your mind is trying to help you.

The main point we are trying to make is that all the examples just given are thoughts. They are just words in your head. You may disregard all of them. You may engage with all of them. It really comes down to whether doing what the thought suggests would be consistent with your values. It is possible to build up the skill of listening to your thoughts when you need to and disregarding them when they're not useful. In this chapter, we will help you build this skill.

Why Do Certain Thoughts Hook Us?

Minds produce thousands of thoughts every day. They have an opinion about everything. Just look around wherever you are. We bet your mind has a thought on everything. That is just fine. That is what minds do. We are good at ignoring the bulk of the thoughts that we have. But we each have our big thoughts, the thoughts that hook us and pull us in. For some it's around weight or looks, a fear of germs, or worry about their family.

You likely have some thoughts that really hook you, that feel compelling and important, about getting things, your belongings, what they say about you, and why you shouldn't discard things. Recognizing the thoughts that grab you will help you know which ones you need to work on responding to in a different way. Here is a list of thoughts that are common for people who struggle with acquiring and saving.

- *This item makes me who I am. Losing it would mean losing part of my identity.*
- *I'll forget an important memory if I let this go.*
- *I'll forget to do something I need to do if I let this go or put it out of sight.*
- *Throwing things out/giving things away is wasteful.*
- *I'm responsible for my items and I need to make sure they are used in the best possible way.*
- *This item is a unique opportunity to learn or do something; if I don't get the item I'll miss out on something meaningful.*
- *This item needs to go to a good home where it'll be loved/appreciated.*

- *It would be too sad to leave an item that needs a home.*
- *Letting go of this item would be devastating.*
- *I'll lose important information if I discard or organize this.*
- *This item is unique and irreplaceable.*
- *Throwing out an item would feel like hurting a person.*
- *I don't want anyone else touching or using my things.*

As we already noted, you can't stop thinking these thoughts. The power of these thoughts may lessen over time if you give them less attention, but they will never stop entirely. As an analogy, if we asked you your childhood phone number or address, you probably remember it even though you may not have used it for dozens of years. Once a certain thought is in your head, it's not really possible to pull it out by the roots and ensure it will never come up again.

Arguing against the thought tends to just give your mind more opportunities to come up with creative ways to defend it—if you're the family member of someone with hoarding, this is one reason why we strongly recommend you avoid putting yourself in the position of trying to convince your loved one their reasons to save items are inaccurate. Thus, what is important is not to remove or fight these thoughts, but to make room for them when they show up, recognize them for what they are, and make decisions that are based on who you want to be rather than what you are thinking.

Our clients usually have a few thoughts that are especially compelling. For example, when we worked with Marco (chapter 2) on decluttering, he could let go of some thoughts easily. If he had the thought, *Maybe I'll reread my old college textbooks someday*, he could pretty easily notice that he hadn't revisited his textbooks before and had no need to now, and recognize that the thought wasn't useful. But his thoughts about waste were really different, and he truly believed them and thought they were accurate when they came up. If the thought arose that "I can't get rid of my old college textbooks because there might be someone out there who can make use of them, and I'm responsible for finding that person," he really believed it and would find himself defending that thought.

But you can believe something and not act on it. This happens all day long. You think a task at work is pointless, yet you do it anyway. Your neighbor shares some obnoxious political belief, and you think you ought to tell him off, but you choose not to. Even if your thought is totally accurate, you do not have to do what it says. Although Marco found it very challenging, he chose to recycle most of his old college textbooks even while having the thought that it was wasteful.

Ways to Recognize Sticky Thoughts and Let Them Go

You have thousands of thoughts a day. You only act on hundreds of them, and you generally ignore the bulk of them. That means you are not responding to thousands of thoughts a day. Most of these are silly little thoughts that are easy to let go. Maybe some of them grab you a little bit and it is a bit harder to let them go. Transitioning to the thoughts that you act on, we would argue that a handful of them enrich your life, a bunch of them are neutral, and a handful cause problems in your life. In our experience it can be difficult to set rules around which thoughts are "good" and which ones are "bad."

The reason this is difficult is that it's really a matter of what situation you're in. For example, we cannot tell you whether you should listen to the thought, "I should save this." The situation you're in, and your experiences when you followed that thought in past circumstances, will answer that question. If you try to really scrutinize thoughts about whether you should save something, you could find yourself arguing back and forth for hours without getting anywhere, because again, your mind is an incredible thinking machine.

Our minds can be a bit like a young child who keeps asking "why," or "what if," or "how do you know for sure?" It is constantly seeking coherence; it needs a story that makes sense. Consequently, we might feel like we cannot act until we have a "good" reason. Yet, there are very few decisions in life where we can be completely positive of the right answer. Your mind can keep you stuck in that grey space by continually asking, "yeah, but what if?"

The skill that we want to develop is the ability to notice what your mind is saying, recognize the situation that you're in, and then make a *choice*. A *choice* is picking among multiple options. Sometimes people contrast it with a *decision* which is much more like weighing all the options and thinking through everything to come to the perfect answer.

Try making some choices about your belongings—to keep or discard them, or where to put something—in a relatively quick period, and then follow through. If it's at all possible, do this right now. If your mind is fighting back right now that it can't work that way, just thank it for doing its job. Your mind probably does not like what we're saying because it's different than what you usually do. And if you aren't already feeling uncomfortable, chances are pretty good that you will after actually following through on this kind of choice. But don't forget, if the way you did it worked well, you probably would not have picked up this book. Learning some new skills might be the right move. Feeling uncomfortable, in the service of taking your life in new directions, might open up possibilities that are not available while feeling certain and comfortable.

One of the clients we mentioned in chapter 2, Judith, loved books and had a large collection of many different types of books, in boxes and piles all over her home. She kept every book she had read, had received many as gifts, and used to buy lots of books from her library's book sale. She felt a strong sense of affection toward her book collection, but recognized that she had far more books than she really had space for. When we first encouraged Judith to try making a prompt choice—rather than a drawn-out decision—about whether to keep or donate her books, she found it overwhelming. She felt upset and said she didn't want to be "careless" about books.

We asked her to tune in and identify the thoughts coming up that made this feel so hard. She noticed that the thoughts she kept getting stuck on were about missed opportunities (like, "Maybe this book will have some new insight that will help me turn my life around—I'd feel terrible if I missed out on a book I could have benefited from") and regret ("I spent so much money at the book sale each year—if I get rid of these books now it's like that was all a big mistake"). As she noticed those thoughts coming up repeatedly, she saw how much those thoughts pulled her in and bossed her around, and she recognized that she couldn't make the changes she wanted if she was going to keep listening to those thoughts.

While she continued to find those thoughts unpleasant, she got more and more comfortable making a choice about each book quickly and sometimes making choices that weren't controlled by those thoughts. For instance, she gave away self-help books about better relationships despite having some thoughts that she might miss out on useful information. As she practiced this new way of decluttering, she was struck by how she had been really scared she would feel regret, but instead, mostly felt liberated and relieved.

To sum up, we want you to try making choices about your things with your thoughts along for the ride, but not necessarily in the driver's seat. As you do so, you may find that your mental rules change about your belongings, about what's important, and about your emotions. You may also feel more freedom not to follow your rules all the time, even if they don't change. But all of this starts with making different choices—if you stay on the same path and listen to your thoughts in just the same way as always, there's not much room to change.

Your Attention

We mentioned before that your mind is made to scan for danger, to forecast the future, and to solve problems. This doesn't just affect your thinking, but also your attention. You probably pay attention to potential dangers or watch for things that could go wrong without even thinking about it. If you walk or drive around a city, you attend to the vehicles around you or someone approaching. If you have a problem to solve, like running late, your mind might be looking for ways to solve your problem, scanning for openings in traffic or possible shortcuts. Your attention might also be drawn toward things that could be pleasant or rewarding, like noting ads for deliciously sugary coffee drinks.

Your attention is drawn to certain things for good reasons: to keep you safe, solve problems, and seek out rewarding things. But these predispositions in our attention don't always benefit us. In a situation that poses no threat we can find the one unhappy look on a friend's face, or the one yawn, and judge ourselves for being boring. It is well documented that people with phobias can more quickly pick out the things they're phobic of, or places where a threat may be, than someone without a phobia.

Similarly, we would predict that someone who focuses on acquiring and saving has a special attention to those types of items. So instead of being out and appreciating what is going on around you, the interesting people, the different sights and smells, your attention may be on items that are worth acquiring.

But the amazing thing about being a human being is that our attention does not even need to be on things that are in front of us. We can attend to things that have happened in the past (rumination) or plot and plan about things that may happen in the future (worry). So even if the present moment is actually quite nice, we can ponder the mistake that we made a couple days ago, or the future issues we might be in, and predict and plan ways to solve them.

EXERCISE: Your Mind as a Pie Chart

Take out a piece of paper or a journal if you use one. We are going to give you five categories to think about where you may put your attention: *the distant past, the recent past, right now, the near future, the distant future.*

We think of the *distant past* as a couple months or greater, and this might include thinking about memories or mistakes from a long time ago. The *recent past* would include thinking about what you've been doing or events that have occurred at least a few minutes ago and up to a few weeks ago. *The near future* might include worrying, planning, and preparing for things in the next days or weeks. *The distant future* is picturing and thinking about things months or years away. *Right now* refers to being in the present and having your attention fully focused on what is there, what you are sensing or doing in this moment. It is possible to be a little bit in the future and a little bit in the present so we're really asking you where you are placing most of your attention in a given moment.

Focusing on those five categories (distant past, recent past, right now, near future, distant future), in a general day what percentage of your attention is put into each one of those categories? If you add these, they should equal 100 percent. If you're somebody who ruminates a lot, much of your attention is probably in the distant or recent past. If you're someone who worries a lot, you would have quite a bit of time in the near future or distant future. For most people it takes effort to truly be in the present moment.

Take a second and ponder your results. How do you feel about this? Is this how you want it to be? Does this feel like something you should work on? Usually, people can identify that *right now* is a small slice of the pie—so maybe the typical person spends 50 percent of their time focused on the *near future*, 10 percent on the *distant future*, 20 percent on the *near past*, 10 percent on the *distant past*, and just 10 percent on *right now*. Because our minds are planning, predicting, and problem-solving machines, they often pull our attention out of the present.

When your attention gets pulled into the past or the future, it's often because a thought has popped up in your mind.

Sometimes it may be easy to dismiss a thought or memory and return to the present, but at other times the thought may feel really weighty and capture your attention. For example, when Nicole, our client who had been through a separation, started to think about how different her life was a few years ago and how many things had gone wrong for her, she would often end up spending hours mulling over her past. Notice if there are any particular thought patterns that tend to pull your attention out of the present.

Bringing Your Attention to This Moment

We have found in research that difficulty attending to the present contributes to problems with acquiring and discarding things. For example, you might pick up new items without even realizing it, acting out of habit and sort of running on autopilot. Or your mind might focus so much on future uses of an object that you miss the fact that keeping the object is creating problems for you now and you really haven't needed it. Or your mind might skip over the clutter in your house, not noticing how big certain piles have gotten or the problems they are creating, or things that you could let go of.

Alternatively, you may have big plans to declutter in the future—when your kids are out of school, or when you have more energy—and yet that future time never quite seems to come, and you do not act right now because you're planning for the "right" time. Consider this for yourself: how does time spent focusing on the past and future contribute to your challenges with keeping and acquiring things?

The good thing about noticing when your mind shifts to focusing on the past or future is that it also opens up an opportunity—to pause and bring your attention back to the present. In fact, if you only take one thing from this whole chapter it's this simple idea: recognize your mind at work. If you can pause and notice the thoughts going through your mind just for what they are, you'd be surprised how much can change.

Thoughts have power over us primarily when we act on them on autopilot and react to what our mind says, without pausing and noticing it's just our mind doing what it does. If you can recognize your mind and the thoughts it's giving you, you have an opportunity to come back to what you want to focus on and what you want to do that would fit with your values.

Consider what might be different if you could be more present in your life. Maybe you'd be less likely to act out of habit in buying something you see while scrolling online, or more intentional in what you keep or get rid of, or more aware of clutter you want to work on, or find other benefits from just being present more.

There are a lot of ways to practice recognizing your mind at work so you can shift your attention back to the present. We are going to introduce a few right now that we find especially helpful. They are all designed to be quick so you can use them in the moment when you catch you aren't present, and you can quickly shift back to the present.

EXERCISE: Shifting to the Present

We encourage you to briefly try each of these ways to shift your attention to the present now and then pick one you want to focus on practicing throughout your week—maybe writing them down on a note or your phone to remember.

- **Label the thoughts.** Note the thoughts your mind is giving you by simply adding the label "I'm having the thought that..." to whatever you are thinking. For example, "I'm having the thought that I have to go to the store later." Notice the gaps in thinking that sometimes come after labeling thoughts so you can shift attention back to what is happening here and now. You can also just say "thinking" in your head with each thought that grabs your attention.

- **Notice three things.** There are so many things happening in the present and pausing to notice a variety of experiences can help center you in the here and now. The idea with this exercise is to take a moment to notice three things in your current space (big and obvious or small and subtle, and ideally something new you hadn't noticed). We recommend trying this with a few different senses—so noticing three things you can hear, then three things you can see, and three things you can feel in your body. Just taking a moment to notice different experiences that are present.
- **Committing to one activity.** Our lives generally don't support being present, and one of the biggest examples of this is the pull to multitask (admittedly, one of us is eating a snack while writing this statement). Focusing on doing just one thing can be an excellent way to slow down and be present. For this skill, pick an activity and commit to limiting distractions while focusing your attention just on what you are doing in this one activity. You can pick something small and short—washing a few dishes, taking a brief walk, enjoying tea, and so on. As you do the activity, notice if your mind wanders to the past or future, and when it does, simply note it and bring your attention back to what you are doing. You might have to do this every few moments, and that's okay. It's not about preventing your mind from wandering, it's about noticing when it does and being able to shift back to the present.

Attention Is Different for Different People

We all vary in terms of how difficult it is to focus and keep our attention on the present, and for some people this can be especially difficult. Many people with hoarding problems also have ADHD, or otherwise struggle to focus. It may feel like your mind jumps all over the place. The important part of shifting to the present is practicing and taking the opportunity to notice when your mind pulls you away. There's a famous phrase in mindfulness: "If you go away 1000 times, come back 1000 times."

If your mind is especially scattered, it's helpful to start by limiting potential distractions while practicing one of these skills. When you practice one of the previous skills (or if you do other mindfulness exercises) we recommend practicing at first in a relatively quiet place with your phone turned off and where others won't likely interrupt you. You can also set a timer for however long you want to practice so you don't keep checking the clock and instead can just stay in the present till your alarm goes off. The most important thing is to remember to be patient and kind to yourself because it's hard to slow down and focus on the present. You will get distracted, and that's sort of the point—to simply notice when this happens and return to the present.

Putting This into Practice

The next step is to use these skills to help you notice and navigate challenging thoughts as you work on decluttering. When you start decluttering, or thinking about decluttering, your mind will likely kick into high gear providing worries, doubts, excuses, and other reasons you shouldn't get rid of things. Your job is to simply notice all these thoughts as thoughts, while continuing with your choice to declutter. Let's work on setting up a goal to practice this week with decluttering. We will walk you through some skills we find can be especially helpful for sticking to your choices, even when your mind tries to tell you not to.

EXERCISE: Watch Your Mind Get Busy

Pick a challenging situation with decluttering where your mind gets loud and tries to get you to stop one way or another. Pick something you'd be willing to do this week even though it's hard—maybe going through bills, spending twenty minutes organizing a closet, going through a box in the garage, taking some items for donation, or whatever fits your goals for decluttering. Once you have this challenging decluttering situation in mind, continue on.

When you are decluttering in this challenging situation (or thinking about decluttering in this situation), the first skill is to notice your thoughts and what they are telling you to do. This is one of the most powerful things you can do, which is why we call this chapter *recognizing your mind at work*. Practicing this can take rules you must live by and how the world works, and shift them into what they actually are: ideas, beliefs, and predictions from your mind that may or may not be true, and may or may not be helpful to focus on. Sometimes it's hard to notice the thoughts that we get pushed around by, maybe because we've had such a long habit of just acting on them.

One thing that can help is to notice when strong emotions come up as you work on sorting and decluttering—emotions like anxiety, guilt, or sadness. Emotions can be a signal of thoughts that really hook you, so see if you can slow down and tune into what you are thinking—Why is this action so hard to take? What are you afraid will happen?

Try to notice the thoughts and emotions that come up, not as a problem that has to be solved, but simply as a part of your experience right now. Answers to questions like these can help you to notice the thoughts that you are getting hooked by. If you still feel stuck, you might start with guesses like "What would someone else think if they were in this situation?" or "What might I be thinking if I was just to guess?"

See if you can set an intention to just observe whatever thoughts come up for you. Your job isn't to steer the thoughts you have, argue with them, change them, or act on them. It's just to watch them for a bit and notice them simply for what they are—thoughts your mind is giving you. For example, you might pick up an object you are considering getting rid of, and then just watch what your mind does and all the thoughts that flow by.

Making Use of Your Mind

Noticing your thoughts can give you the space to make your own choice, even if your mind is being pushy. This is different from working through your thoughts till you come to the best decision. Instead, it's about choosing to do what is important and meaningful to you, even if your mind doesn't like it.

To make effective choices about your belongings, you might want to consider different reasons to keep something or to let it go, like whether you have the space for it, how often you use it, how many things like it you have, and so on. But try to use those thoughts and considerations like tools for making a choice rather than a set of rules you must follow. As you consider choices, it can help to come back to your values (what is important and meaningful to you) and also reflect on your experience (what has worked well and not so well in your life).

When your mind is getting bossy about a choice and what you should do, take a moment and ask yourself, "What usually happens when I do what my mind says in a situation like this, and does that work for my goals and values?" Marco started asking himself this question when it came to his half-finished projects. He noticed that his mind complained loudly anytime he considered discarding or even organizing items from incomplete projects, insisting that he both had to finish the projects and would definitely get around to them soon. But when he checked this against his experience, he could notice that his experience was that he would rarely come back to these projects and that the number of incomplete projects had only increased over time. The goal here is to look to what your experience tells you in making a choice, rather than what your mind is saying you should do.

It is important to stick with your choice, even if your mind gets really busy and upset about it. This is so important because if you are doing things differently in your life, your mind will probably not like it, and so your mind will work hard to convince you to go back to your usual patterns and undo changes.

If you immediately go back on your actions, for example by keeping your "discard" box in your home in case you change your mind, then you won't ever have the chance to see if doing something different leads to better outcomes for you. So we recommend making a commitment to sticking with a choice for some time before looking back at it and how it worked.

Let's take an example to show what we mean. After Marco donated some tools that he had bought for a model train project but never gotten around to using, he kept thinking about all of the different things he could have done with the tools, and the times in the past when he had gotten rid of tools and then ended up needing them. He was seriously considering going to the thrift store to see if they had put out the things he donated. But after he stuck with his commitment for several days, he found that those thoughts that he had to go and find the tools no longer seemed so pressing and urgent. And as time ticked on, he never needed those tools.

So, we encourage you to keep your commitment and to watch what happens with curiosity. You likely will have doubts about whether you made the right choice and if you should do something to undo your actions (go back and get the object you threw away, find another one to buy online, etc.). When you choose to do something different and your mind gets busy like this, what if you treat it like an experiment?

What we mean is that your mind is making a lot of predictions about what is going to happen and what will go wrong if you don't have the items. But if you just act on that thought (for example, rebuying what you got rid of), you'll never know if your choice would have turned out well, and instead you'll be stuck in the same pattern you have been in that hasn't been working well. An experiment means waiting a while to see what actually happens when you stick with your choice. If it didn't work well, now you know and you can approach the situation differently next time. But the only way to know is to stick with your choice and see what happens.

What's Next?

Altogether these skills amount to practicing the following when you are working on decluttering in a challenging situation where your mind gets loud: notice your thoughts, check your thoughts against your experience, make a choice, and treat it like an experiment as you stick with your choice. With that in mind, think of a goal you can commit to with decluttering this week. If you can, write it down somewhere you will see it to help remember. This might include 1) something you want to work on with decluttering that brings up difficult thoughts, 2) how you will work on noticing thoughts, and 3) what you are choosing to commit to in that situation (for example, throwing out an object even if your mind says you shouldn't). Your mind may not like it, but let's see if that helps you meet your goals.

CHAPTER 6

Letting Go of the Push and Pull

Let us ask you a question. When you think of emotions such as frustration, anxiety, desire, sadness, do you see these as good, neutral, or bad emotions? Most people rate these as bad emotions. Some feel quite strongly about this, while others lean a bit toward neutral, but deep down they don't prefer these emotions. In all our work, we've never met anybody who likes these emotions.

Why do people rate emotions this way? We would argue it's just basic socialization. As we are growing up, and we experience versions of these emotions, the adults who are taking care of us teach us that there is something wrong with these emotions and that we should work to get rid of them.

To get rid of these emotions, we do the logical things clever people would do. We work hard, we go to therapists, we take medications, we procrastinate, we talk about it to our friends and talk to ourselves in our heads. In the case of clutter, you might have an area of your home that is in need of decluttering. When you think about that area you feel overwhelmed. Then, to help regulate that feeling, you put this out of your mind and focus on other things.

The same could be true for acquiring. You see something of value, and you feel guilt or excitement about getting that item. Instead of passing that item and feeling the guilt of leaving it, you calm that guilt by putting it in your trunk. You might even calm the secondary guilt by telling yourself you will donate it. The truth is most people do a lot of things to regulate feelings they have deemed negative. Some people make it their full-time job to regulate feelings they don't like. Some people work more hours than a full-time job trying to regulate their emotions.

The Limits of Control

If we stop and look at your success in trying to regulate thoughts and emotions, our guess is that you will see that you're not very good at it. You may be good at controlling how you feel for minutes, but we doubt you've ever been able to control how you feel for days or longer. Test this idea out. What emotions are you keeping at bay by holding onto your stuff? Is it about worry, grief, anger, embarrassment, uncertainty, or something else? What emotions are you clinging to? Perhaps excitement, joy, hope, nostalgia, comfort, security.

Our guess is that when you're feeling overwhelmed, you have things you can do to make yourself feel less overwhelmed for a brief while. Maybe you look at your items and make a plan. Maybe you tell yourself you are helping. It is also possible you talk to someone and they make you feel "better." Regardless, these are all relatively quick fixes. The feeling of overwhelm will likely be back later in the day or the next day. Holding onto a feeling is much the same—maybe getting a new item or scoring an amazing bargain feels great for a few minutes, or an hour, but probably not much longer.

Whatever feelings you've been avoiding by holding onto items have probably become more central and intense over time, rather than smaller and easier. Internal experiences like emotions respond just like people or animals do to how we interact with them. If you give the feeling attention and do what the feeling "wants" you to do, it will come back. The more you poke and prod at it, the more important it becomes in your life. The more attention you give it, the more it'll ask for attention. After Judith (chapter 2) inherited her parents' things, she felt overwhelmed and sad when she looked at them. She took her mind off these feelings by focusing on other people in her life, or by zoning out and watching TV a lot, and sometimes by drinking a second or third glass of wine. But avoiding her distress just made it feel bigger and more central.

Maybe you are someone who looks at the "free" section in online marketplaces. Our bet is that the more you have looked at these sites, the more your desire and interest to look at these sites has increased. Interest in these sites occurred, you reinforced it, and it has grown. Getting the things you want hasn't worked to decrease your desire, but only made it larger.

In a way, how emotions work is really counterintuitive. In many areas of life, when we don't like something, we can work hard and change it. If you need a haircut, you can get one. If the brakes on your car are squeaking, you can take them in to get worked on. But if you are feeling overwhelmed and frustrated, you can't just work hard and make that go away. Actually, the harder you work to make those feelings go away, the bigger they become.

We know, this is a bummer. But there's a good part about this too. If we know that strong attempts to regulate thoughts and emotions are like throwing kindling on a fire, that also tells us that we must develop other strategies to deal with strong thoughts and emotions. It's good to know how the world really works. If controlling your emotions isn't possible, and trying to control them only backfires, you don't have to organize your life around controlling or changing how you feel. You don't have to keep working harder to feel confident, or secure, or calm, or happy.

As we worked with Judith, she started to notice that she was waiting to stop feeling so overwhelmed before she decluttered, or got back into hobbies, or reached out to her friends. Recognizing that she could not make the overwhelmed feeling go away was absolutely terrifying at first. But when she really acknowledged it, she understood that there was no point in waiting for it to go away before she started living her life, and she started taking small steps to do the things she really wanted.

In this next section of the book, we are going to help you develop more functional ways to respond to your internal experiences, especially around saving and acquiring. It's going to be a little bit of a rollercoaster because it's different than what you've been doing. If you are like anyone we've worked with, a lot of your life has been organized around controlling how you feel and keeping in your comfort zone, and we're here to teach you how to reorient your life around doing what matters while relinquishing the demand for control and comfort. But if what you've been doing got you to where you are, it's probably time to try something new.

The Role of Thoughts, Feelings, and Sensations

Let's apply these ideas to saving and acquiring. Think about what happens for you when you look at a collection of things in your home that you know needs to be cleaned up in some way. Our guess is that if you purchased this book there are many examples of this in your home.

EXERCISE: Notice What Comes Up Inside

Pick one pile of newspapers, magazines, old electronics, or items from a past phase of your life that you still have. Picture where it is in your house. How many items are there? What are they? Now in your mind, picture really cleaning up that area in a reasonable amount of time. What we mean by a reasonable amount of time is that you do not get to spend multiple days or weeks going through this collection of material; you must go through these things and quickly choose what to do with them.

What thoughts, feelings, or bodily sensations are showing up for you as you picture cleaning out this area? Are you having thoughts about not knowing the right thing to do? Are you thinking "it's not fair I have to get rid of these wonderful items?" Are you thinking "People don't understand how important this is?" Are you feeling tension, frustration, or anxiety? In terms of bodily sensations, did your heart start beating faster, did your stomach feel a little bit upset, and do you feel a bit of tension throughout your body? Take at least five minutes to sit and notice what comes up for you.

Our assumption is that reducing clutter in your house is associated with all sorts of internal experiences that you find upsetting. This may be a factor that a lot of people around you do not appreciate. It is hard for you to just go clean out these areas. There are a lot of emotions and thoughts tied to this work. And if you avoid this work then you also get to avoid dealing with these emotions.

In general, people are attuned to the "negative" emotions that they feel around acquiring and saving. They generally pay less attention to the "positive" emotions that they feel when finding an item or when looking through their items. Next, let's do a similar exercise to the one we did with the difficult emotions in the previous paragraph.

EXERCISE: Notice the Positives

We would like you to think about a time when you found something exciting or meaningful and were able to either take it home or to a better place. Maybe you had something in your home for a long time and then you finally found someone who wanted or needed it. For example, we had a friend who had this old motorcycle that was broken but was their grandpa's. It was in the shed for decades. Finally, someone who appreciated it as much as the grandpa bought it and was ready to restore it. That made our friend feel good. They felt a feeling of relief and accomplishment by placing that item. Has this happened for you? If so, what thoughts came along with those moments? What emotion did you feel? Was it excitement, or relief? In terms of bodily sensations, did you feel a sense of calmness or even peace? Take a few minutes to recognize these experiences.

It is common for people who acquire and save to be influenced by emotions they are running from, or what we might call the "negative" ones, and to also be influenced by emotions they enjoy. You are constantly being pushed around by your experiences.

One thing that we encounter when working in psychology is that when a behavior is largely guided by difficult or negative emotions, clients really throw themselves into therapy. When there are strong unpleasant experiences around the clinical issue, clients desire our assistance. We have never met a client who reported enjoying their anxiety, depression, or low self-worth.

But there is a set of disorders that are largely influenced by the client going toward things that they enjoy. These include experiences like a sense of exhilaration during a manic episode, the feelings of euphoria and camaraderie that can go with substance abuse, and the feeling of achievement or excellence that can go with certain types of perfectionism or worry.

It is not hard to imagine how much more difficult it is to shift a behavior that produces thoughts or feelings that the client really enjoys. If you feel that a lot of your hoarding tendencies have to do with positive emotions like joy, excitement, nostalgia, hope, and so on, it might be especially challenging to stay motivated to address your clutter and to let go of some of those positive emotions. At the same time, letting them go may open up opportunities to be the kind of person you want to be. For example, letting go of the comfort that all your books give you might open up the opportunity to start having your loved ones in your home.

The reason we are spending so much time on this, is that we want you to recognize that at all times behavior is being guided by trying to escape emotions we don't like *and* trying to create emotions we do like. It makes complete sense that this is how people work. But there can be times when this way of living can become problematic. We believe that saving and acquiring can be one of these times. Saving and acquiring can cease to be about you following your values and can largely become about ways to regulate your emotions. How you feel is important. It just shouldn't be the director of your life. It will take too much of a toll if it is.

Psychological Acceptance as an Alternative

There is a term in psychology for when controlling emotions takes over your life: experiential avoidance (Hayes et al. 1996). There is nothing inherently wrong with trying to regulate thoughts, feelings, and emotions; there are just times when our attempts to control what we think or feel negatively affect our lives. Most psychological disorders have experiential avoidance at their core, and hoarding is no exception based on research done by us and others (Krafft et al. 2020; Wheaton et al. 2013).

The solution to experiential avoidance is not simple, but one does exist. At a basic level what we are going to ask you to do is to shift decision making from how it feels to do something, to "Is this choice in line with who you want to be?" Basically, it's a shift from experiential avoidance to following values.

This is a little complicated because for most people they look at how they're feeling in deciding to do something. At a simple level it's the difference between letting hunger choose your food or your values around health. We are asking you to not look at how you feel about it, but to more strongly look at what is the choice that aligns with the person you want to be.

The reason we say this is complicated is that you have likely spent a long phase of your life making decisions based on how you feel. Now we are going to ask you to shift how you make decisions to looking at choosing the behaviors that work the best for you. To take up the example of Judith again, she had spent years with how she felt determining whether she decluttered or not. She might discard a few things here or there, but when the sense of being overwhelmed came up, she put off decluttering entirely. Making decisions based on her values meant starting to act very differently, and starting to consistently go through her parents' things even when sadness or fear came up, in pursuit of being a caring and attentive spouse.

Let's make this a bit more real. Picture going into the most cluttered room in your home and removing ten items. Our guess is that the idea of cleaning up 10 items from a room that has 500 items that need cleaning up produces anxiety and frustration. You might even be negatively judging us for suggesting such a "ridiculous" idea. Your mind might be saying, you need a "plan" and you *must* set aside a "couple days." To remove just ten items would produce lots of emotion. Yet if your value is to clean up that room and have a more comfortable space for you and your family, then you are in the trap of either regulating emotions (put it off, make a plan) or following values (cleaning up ten items right now).

When you make a choice based on what is important to you, in that moment, you are still going to be left with those inner experiences that used to push you around. They're going to be standing there waving their arms and kicking and screaming. They are going to be quite annoyed because you have always listened to them.

If you've ever stopped listening to someone, you will know how hard it is for the other person. For example, if you've had a young child who threw tantrums to get what they wanted, and you stopped giving in to the tantrums. There was probably a nice uptick in frustrated and angry behavior when you stopped giving in. In behavior analysis, this is called an extinction burst.

You can try to ignore the emotional reactions you have when you make choices based on your values and goals rather than your feelings. The thing we don't like about ignoring is that ignoring is really saying, "I will not attend to this in the hope that it'll go away." What we encourage you to do is qualitatively different than ignoring. We will call it "openness." This means you are open to experiencing whatever feelings you feel. Openness says, "I will allow these feelings to be here now and later."

The concept of openness is something that we think most of us understand because we show it in all these other places in our lives. We show openness to people who are different. We show openness to people who are having a hard time. We understand that people go through struggles, and we support them during those moments. Let us say a little bit on what being open is like for the person who is doing it. Being open is like being welcoming to a houseguest. You are truly giving the person a space. You might even cook them food they like. You might give them some of your nice drinks, snacks, or bathroom products. You make them feel at home.

Internally, you might not "want" them there. Maybe they annoy you. Yet, it is still possible to be warm to them. That is what we are hoping for with your internal experiences that guide your behavior around your stuff. We want you to appreciate that these emotional "guests" are going to be there and it is partially your job to figure out how to live with them there and not struggle against them on a daily basis. Sometimes we literally acknowledge our feelings, aloud or internally: "Hello shame, I see you, my old companion."

Openness is a compassionate stance. When you show openness to others, by welcoming them just as they are, you are acting with kindness. Because your thoughts and feelings are ultimately a part of you, whether you like them or not, being open to them is a way of acting compassionately toward yourself. Fighting against your feelings involves rejecting a piece of you. Allowing them to be as they are is a form of kindness toward yourself.

Openness Allows Freedom

Clearly, we aren't here to tell you that we have some strategy to make your unwanted thoughts, feelings, or memories go away. Nevertheless, we have some good news for you. The amount of your life that is consumed by urges, thoughts, and bodily sensations can shrink. The way you interact with your internal experiences impacts how often and how intensely they show up. There's nothing we can do to stop them from showing up, but we can impact how central they are to you.

There are some moments in life where the most effective thing you can do is nothing. Anyone who's been a parent knows that sometimes you just have to back off and allow your child to work through their situation. It may not be what we feel like doing internally. Deep down we want to help the child through the difficult situation. But sometimes the best thing we can do is nothing. Internal experiences are like that sometimes. Just like good things can come out of letting your children learn their way through life, good things can come out of allowing your internal experiences to find their place on their own.

The Two Dials

Imagine your emotions being like a machine with two dials. The first dial is how much emotion you are experiencing. The second dial is how open you are to whatever thoughts or feelings are showing up inside your body. The rules are you may only really work on one dial. You can put all your effort into trying to lower your internal experiences. Our history says that this will be a full-time job that you will get to do for the rest of your life.

The other option is that you can focus on making room for the internal experiences that you have as they show up throughout your life. Working on the openness dial will feel strange because it's not the way you've done things. But kind of like letting your child learn some things on their own, sometimes when you just let something be, it kind of figures things out.

If you focus a large amount of your time and energy on regulating your internal experience, it likely enhances the importance of those thoughts and feelings. Those internal experiences become a big part of your life, and your choices start becoming about them. On the flip side, if you focus more heavily on making room for the thoughts and feelings that show up for you throughout the day, the attention goes away from these internal experiences. They become less central and less powerful. They do not go away. They will not go down to zero, but if this felt like carrying ten pounds, it will start to feel more like three or four pounds.

Coming back to Judith, we spent a lot of time working together on increasing her openness. She was so used to putting things off when she felt scared, overwhelmed, or uncertain, that it was essentially automatic. She really struggled with the idea of being open to the emotions that would occur during decluttering, and in conversations with us she would end up listing all the reasons why now was a bad time to try feeling her feelings. We started very small. Judith was willing to pick one small, low-intensity area of her home (like her bathroom medicine cabinet, or one box of odds and ends in her garage) and spend two minutes just looking at it and feeling whatever she felt. She repeated this every day for about two weeks. No pressure to declutter, just noticing her things and being open to her internal experience. The first few times she did this, she felt quite a bit of dread and anxiety, and she really tried to acknowledge it and allow it to be there, despite how unfamiliar that felt.

As she continued, her emotions varied more. Sometimes she felt bored; sometimes she felt excited. A few times, she was surprised by something in the space she had chosen—like noticing one of her mom's old vases in her kitchen cabinet—and felt a rush of intense emotion. After those initial weeks, she was willing to start working on sorting out and discarding items, keeping that open stance. Sometimes she did find herself automatically falling into avoidance, especially when she came across items that provoked a bigger response or reminded her of her childhood, wanting to put off making a decision on them or comfort herself with a drink or distraction. But she noticed how much she had been able to accomplish by working on her home even when she would normally avoid, and she noticed how the feelings of being overwhelmed and scared didn't push her around like they used to.

If we go back to the example of removing 10 things a day from your most cluttered room, our guess is that doing that work will be emotionally hard. Yet, if you do the activity day after day, week after week, you will get better at doing hard things. This is a little different than saying it will get easier. "Easier" implies less internal resistance. You being better at cleaning that room while feeling emotions is a different skill. Nevertheless, it is one you can learn, and if you learn it, then your behavior will be less guided by how you are feeling that day.

Although we've mostly been talking about openness to emotions around decluttering, keep in mind that openness is so much bigger than that. You can practice openness to embarrassment while asking a friend for help or communicating with a family member. You can practice openness to frustration while learning a new skill or interacting with a difficult person in your life. Following your values and being open to the thoughts and feelings that come up while doing so is a recipe for an expansive, rich life.

Let's Practice Openness

In this next section we're going to guide you through a plan of action to practice being open to your internal experiences. To practice we need opportunities that challenge you. Obviously, these challenges are going to be around discarding and reducing acquiring. We have to think at some level you knew this was coming. We need to do the work around the topics that matter to you. If this was a book about social anxiety our examples would be about interacting with new people. If this book was on obsessive-compulsive disorder, we would be talking about approaching your obsessions and allowing them to be there. Because this book is on acquiring and saving, we will be talking about how you respond to your stuff. We have some basic policies on how we structure these practices.

Policy 1. Choose an action that is tied to your values.

At any moment there are probably 100 actions you could take. The list of areas of your house that you could clean out is almost endless. Don't get caught up in choosing the perfect thing, just choose something that you find some meaning in. This could be a task where you can find some purpose in cleaning out this area. Maybe this is a task that you and the person you live with both think would be worthwhile to do. Maybe you can just connect with, "I want to get some work done and grow and this is as good an opportunity as any." The short of it is, we want this work to be about you becoming more of the person you want to be and not something you just have to get through. If you find yourself toughing through this task, pause, and connect with why this is worth doing. In any moment, in any action you're doing, there is an opportunity to connect with something about the activity that means something to you.

Policy 2. Practice being open to your inner experiences while doing the task.

A huge part of this task is practicing being present with the internal experiences that show up while you're working on this. Form matters. If anyone's lifted weights or done physical therapy, you are aware that good form is so much more important than high weight. We would greatly prefer that you pick something small and that you can do with a lot of openness and connection with your values, rather than something gigantic that you are just getting through. One's openness to what's happening inside of them while doing an exercise like this is highly predictive of how much better they'll get in therapy. We really don't want you to power through this task.

Policy 3. Choose an action that is within your ability.

One of us used to say, "Choose something that's embarrassingly easy." We would rather that you do the thing you commit to than commit to something gigantic and not do it. Whatever it is that you pick, we want you to be fully there for this and find this to be a fulfilling growth opportunity. Your mind will say, "You're not doing enough, and this isn't big enough." Just thank your mind for that thought and keep moving. We just want you to engage in tasks that move you forward, no matter how big or how small. There's no speedometer. Nobody is keeping track. You can think of your life like a line on a graph that is either going down, staying steady, or going up. All we ask is that you keep moving in the right direction, even if it's a small percentage per week. Every task makes a difference.

Policy 4. Keep your commitment throughout the whole task.

A wise Jedi once said, "Try not. Do. Or do not. There is no try." While we don't think he was trained in psychotherapy, we do agree with him that the cognitive mindset of, "I'll give it a try," sets one up for failure. Our body is one unit. Trying is really saying, "I will do it until this point, and then I will quit." Your body knows where your cutoff is and will quickly move you to that point. We would rather you choose something within your ability and small enough that you can do it. That way you don't have to enter the task trying to monitor how intense your emotions are. If you choose a task at the right size, you may just begin the task and then complete it. Once the task is over you are welcome to look back at it and contemplate how easy or difficult it was. You may choose whether your next task should be bigger or smaller. But it's key that, whatever task you choose to do, you dive in and do that.

Here are some examples of tasks you could try to sort or discard items:

- Choose one drawer to clean out. Your mind will likely have lots of chatter about the items in that drawer, and "what is the point of cleaning out just one drawer?" Practice just noticing those thoughts and do this task within a tight amount of time (maybe 20-60 minutes).
- Choose ten items to throw out. Again, your mind will have lots of chatter about whether this is the right move or not. This exercise is not only about doing the right thing. It's also about practicing letting your mind yell at you. Also, do this task in a tight amount of time.
- Take one bag of garbage out to the garbage can. Maybe you already have a filled bag or maybe it won't be hard to move around the house and fill one up.
- There could be one large item that you were thinking about donating but haven't done it yet. Take that one item to your donation place and drop it off.
- Maybe you had a set of items you were going to donate somewhere. Do not go through those items again. Pack up that collection and drive them to the donation place.
- Clean off one table or chair.
- Donate or throw away something that you have multiples of. Your mind will tell you that this could be given to a

good home, or that this has some unique value, and part of this exercise is learning to just allow those types of thoughts and let them come and go.

- Ask a loved one where they see one of the biggest problems in the house and choose a project there.

EXERCISE

Go ahead and choose one action that you will take that involves sorting or discarding items, while practicing openness. It can be from the list above or adapted. We encourage you to do this right now if possible, or if needed, you can plan a time to do it in the next couple days and give yourself some type of reminder.

Reducing Acquiring

There are two things you need to work on in this area. The first one is slowly moving items out of your home, and the second one is bringing in fewer items. Only you know which one will have a bigger impact on your life. At the low end of acquiring, there are people who only acquire items when presented with a unique opportunity. These people may go weeks at a time without really bringing in anything notable. But when presented with an opportunity such as things from someone's home they cared about, or passing a nice sale, they can acquire large amounts.

There are other people who have regular rotations of looking for valuable items. These could be people who drive around on garbage day, attend estate or garage sales, or frequent resale stores. There are also people who shop for bargains or purchase new items online. As we've noted in this book, there is nothing inherently problematic with enjoying acquiring. But for some people there is a tipping point where too much is happening and it's causing a problem in their lives. Only you know where this is. Given that you have this book in your hand there's probably been some realization that you've acquired too much.

We would like you to use the same general principles in reducing your acquiring as we already mentioned. You may need to look at how much you're generally acquiring or some of the patterns of acquiring that you maintain. Maybe you need to make commitments to lessen that frequency.

1. Connect with why it is important to you to make this change. What is the value behind altering your behavior? Use that value to motivate you.

2. When you choose to not acquire something, a set of thoughts and feelings will show up and try to get you to change your mind. Use your skills of openness and stepping back and just notice what your mind is saying. If you get caught in a fight with your mind, work on following your values over your mind's logic.

3. When you make your overall commitment, choose something that you will easily do. If you're someone who drives around for a couple hours a day checking the garbage, reduce that by an hour. If you're someone who maybe brings home about twenty new items a week, cut that down to fifteen.

4. Whatever you pick, treat it like it's the law. If you say you're bringing home only fifteen items per week and you got there quickly, then just treat it like it is impossible to bring home any more items. Do not negotiate with your mind at these times. The mind does not play fairly. Here

are some examples of behavior changes we have seen around acquiring.

- Setting a particular number of items that may be brought home within a week.
- Setting a particular amount of time that may be spent acquiring per week.
- Setting a particular amount of time shopping, or amount of money spent on shopping.
- Creating policies around how much can be acquired in certain categories (e.g., only buying a new soap after using one up, or buying no more than five clothing items per month).
- Making a list of the things that are needed for the following week and rigidly adhering to that list.

Chapter 7 will also talk more about strategies that may help you to reduce acquiring.

EXERCISE

Go ahead and choose one guideline you're willing to adopt to reduce acquiring while practicing openness. It can be from the list above or adapted. Start using it right now. If you decide, "No more than $20 spent on thrift store clothing this week," start following this rule right away rather than deciding you'll start at another time.

What's Next?

If this was a lot to take in, please show yourself some patience and kindness. You are doing the work. We never said it was going to be simple. Most things that are worthwhile take effort. Just keep moving. Put one foot in front of the other. We will keep working on practical steps to reduce clutter and the number of items you are bringing in throughout the next chapter.

CHAPTER 7

Decluttering and Organizing Effectively

When we treat hoarding, we focus a lot on disentangling from unhelpful thoughts, allowing the full spectrum of emotions, and cultivating robust sources of meaning and purpose. But hoarding is also a bit of a unique psychological disorder in that it requires you to literally roll up your sleeves and get to work to address it. So, while all of this book is designed to be practical, this chapter in particular focuses on the nitty-gritty, brass-tacks aspects of organizing and decluttering, now that you know a bit more about what to do with the internal stuff.

There are a seemingly endless number of decluttering and organizing "systems" out there, promising unbelievable results if you buy their book, download their app, get their subscription, etc. Chances are good that you've already tried some of them. They may be helpful for you, or they may not.

There's a general trap that is really easy to fall into when trying to address hoarding or really making any other kind of big behavior change. You try to find the perfect system, the perfect solution, and then you look for just the right time to implement it. You wait until you feel ready, until you have more energy, until the next summer break, or until after your kids are a bit bigger—whatever it might be.

But the perfect moment doesn't come, the fully prepared version of you never emerges, and the perfect system either doesn't get implemented at all or rapidly falls apart. So, what are you to do? In essence, find a good-enough system, a good-enough approach, and start now, exactly as you are. A good-enough method for decluttering and organizing needs to have two essential features: you are able and willing to do it regularly, and it leads to measurable improvement. Chapter 4 talks about these aspects in more detail, so you may want to revisit it if you find yourself struggling to figure out what a good-enough approach involves for you.

We're going to lay out some strategies and methods for organizing and decluttering in this chapter, and as you read through them, or try them out, try to keep this broader perspective in mind. You don't need to find a perfect system; you need to find a good-enough method and put it in place.

Finding Time

This is by no means unique to hoarding, but most people with hoarding have every intention of cleaning up their home and just haven't found the time. This is understandable—we have yet to meet a thoughtful adult human who feels like they have enough time for everything important in their lives. Our time is finite. Much of it is given over to work or caregiving or other activities that are both essential and not fully in our control.

In Oliver Burkeman's *Four Thousand Weeks: Time Management for Mortals*, he notes that "it's painful to confront how limited your time is, because it means that tough choices are inevitable and that you won't have time for all you once dreamed you might do." So, if you feel like you don't have enough time to declutter, you're probably right! At the same time, none of us have enough time for all the things that are deeply important to us, and acknowledging this reality can be liberating. (Burkeman's book, by the way, is excellent and has influenced our thinking below about time-related dilemmas).

What should you do if decluttering is really important *and* you don't have enough time for it? First off, this dilemma means you have no choice but to prioritize. If decluttering is going to happen, you need to choose spending your time on it above other things. If you wait to declutter until everything else is done—you've responded to every email, done all the yard work, exercised, called your friends, done all your work or homework or other obligations, and so on—you will never get to it. So if decluttering is important, think about what it should be prioritized *over*. Consider this: what is one thing you routinely spend time on that is less important than decluttering?

We also highly recommend focusing on consistency. If you're waiting for your next vacation, or when the kids are back in school, or when the kids are out of school, or the kids go to college, or when you retire, to declutter—in our experience, this tends not to work out well. On the one hand, we're not going to lie, it absolutely is easier to declutter when you have more time. On the other hand, life is unpredictable. Maybe that vacation finally comes and you're sick that week. Maybe you hit retirement, and then soon after a loved one has a medical problem and needs lots of help from you. Right now is the only time we are guaranteed, so it's generally better to think about what you can realistically and consistently do than wait for the right time.

Also, when you start to really recognize and acknowledge how limited your time is, it makes some things way easier. Nicole could maintain the illusion that she was going to sell all the clothes sitting in her bedroom as long as she just kept putting it off and waiting for the right moment to come. When she started actually working on it, bit by bit, and noticed how long it really takes to list and sell and ship items of clothing, she got to scrutinize her plans under the harsh light of reality and realize she would never be able to sell them all. While this was frustrating and disappointing for her, it was also freeing, because she was now prepared to just donate the clothes and get them out of her space.

Ways to Discard

The fundamental task in addressing hoarding is to look through your items, sort them into items to keep or discard, organize the ones you're keeping, and dispose of the ones you aren't. Everything below is a variation on this basic task. You identify a chunk of stuff, and start sorting.

The Basics

When sorting, you can try just making a "keep" and "discard" pile. Sometimes people find a "maybe" pile helpful, but if you use one, keep an eye to make sure it's effective for you and makes it easier to discard over time rather than fueling procrastination and avoidance. You may need more piles depending on how you're letting go of belongings (e.g., trash, recycling, donating to a thrift store, posting to an online group, selling, giving to a friend). Having too many categories can bog you down, so we suggest you try using the smallest number of categories that works for you. For items you're keeping, you may want to sort them into boxes or bags by category (e.g., sorting clothing, papers, and food into separate bags).

Once a decision is made, try to implement it as soon as reasonably possible. Try to put the "keep" items into their final destination in your home (or a box/bag close by) right away and build time into your plan for this step. For items leaving your home, get them in the trash or recycling right away if you can, or try to donate/post them within a week. This will keep you from losing track of the decisions you made and having to repeat your hard work. Our client, Judith, really struggled with this. She would get into a groove sorting belongings and neatly bagging up items that she planned to drop off at a thrift store. But each week, we would show up and those bags were right where they had been when we left.

We explored what got in the way of putting them in her car and dropping them off, and Judith noticed a well-worn, habitual thought pattern that handing them over meant facing the chance that she had accidentally put something in there that she didn't mean to and wouldn't be able to get it back. When we asked Judith if having that space in her home would be worthwhile enough for her to allow that feeling of uncertainty, and the possibility of making a mistake, she decided that it absolutely was, and she dropped the bags off that week.

Make sure your methods for discarding are realistic for you. Marco wanted to downsize his collection of sci-fi but was only willing to let books go if he could identify a specific person to give them to that he knew would enjoy them. Because he had set such a high bar for discarding the books, it was nearly impossible to make any notable progress. He ultimately had to find a more realistic method (sending them to an online used bookstore) to make the progress he wanted. If you plan to sell items, make sure you have the time to sell them and that the money you get from selling them is worth the time and effort it requires of you.

Another trap that's worth keeping an eye out for is what gets called "churning." This is a pattern that people with hoarding often fall into, especially if you have trouble making decisions. You go through a pile of items and sort them, but nothing—or very little—actually gets discarded.

Instead, as you go through the pile, you're reminded of why you got that item in the first place, or you have an idea for how you might use it, or you just aren't sure about it—these thoughts take your attention away from the task at hand. You might then relocate a bunch of items—putting articles you don't want to forget on top of another pile, or moving mail into a "revisit" pile, but in the end, you have basically the same amount of stuff, and it's not much more organized than before. If you want to go from a hoarded home to an organized one, there's no getting around making decisions and actually taking stuff out of your home, so keep an eye to make sure that any method you use makes that more likely rather than less likely.

Below, we describe some more specific strategies for sorting and discarding items. Read through them, and choose one or two things to try out.

General Rules

Identifying a few rules that work to help guide your decision making can be very helpful. One common strategy has to do with timeframes, for example, *If I haven't used this item in the past five years, I don't need it.* Choosing a few guiding questions for discarding can also be helpful, such as asking yourself if you love this item, how often you use it, how hard it would be to replace, or whether you would buy it again if you saw it in a store. Watch for falling into a rabbit hole of the mind; these questions should be tools to serve you, not feel like you're putting your attachments on trial.

Boundary/Container Method

There are a few more specific strategies you can try out for sorting and discarding. One is what's called the "boundary method" or "container concept" popularized by Dana K. White (2018). In this method, you choose a container for a specific category of items, then only keep items that fit in that container. This can be a literal container. Let's say you're a knitter and have too much yarn. Using this method, you would choose one container of reasonable size, then sort through all the yarn you have, putting in your favorites until the container is full. Whatever's left is then discarded. The container or boundary can be larger or less literal too. For example, decluttering your books until they fit onto the bookcases you currently own, or decluttering your sweaters until they fit on one shelf. One thing that some people like about this method is that it causes you to focus on what to keep rather than what to get rid of. You are choosing favorites to keep rather than unnecessary items to toss.

Number Method

Another method of decluttering we've seen people have success with is using a target number and choosing your favorites to keep until you hit that number. Estimate what a reasonable number of towels, or coffee cups, or cookbooks is for your lifestyle and home, and then declutter until you get to that number. This doesn't have to be exact—it can be a useful rule of thumb either way. One client we worked with said that she thought twenty or thirty T-shirts would be reasonable to own, and as we sorted through the clothes she had throughout her apartment, she would ask herself "Is this one of my top twenty or thirty T-shirts?" then let go of it if not.

Konmari

Marie Kondo's *Konmari* approach to decluttering (Kondo 2014) is one of the most famous methods out there (decluttering methods rarely get their own Netflix show!). In brief, she encourages you to get out every item in a category, then handle every item in that category, check whether it "sparks joy" for you, and keep only the items that spark joy.

Frankly, we think this method is often impractical for people with serious clutter/hoarding problems. If our clients tried to put all their clothing in one pile, it could take days and would probably fill all the (already limited) space in a room, making it very hard to proceed to sorting. Moreover, the exquisite sensitivity to value and charm some people with hoarding have makes it such that anything—even an old receipt—may spark genuine joy. That said, if you find aspects of her approach useful, go for it. Some suggestions she makes, like working from easier to harder categories (saving sentimental items for later on) and focusing on what you want to keep, may be helpful.

Where to Discard Items

We've touched on this briefly, but sometimes people ask about how they can discard items. One option is disposing of them with household garbage or dropping them off at a landfill. This can be done with almost any item, and we'd recommend it for any item that doesn't have clear usefulness or is soiled or broken without an easy fix.

Some items can be recycled, but what and how are very dependent on your local area, so we suggest searching for recycling centers near to you or asking for information about recycling from your local municipality. You may also have options for recycling specialty materials like scrap metal near you, but what they accept varies a lot.

Many thrift stores accept a wide range of donations, and other facilities like schools, homeless shelters, animal shelters, used bookshops, libraries, and churches will accept donations of specific items. Online groups like "Buy Nothing" groups can be helpful for giving away items, and people in these groups will often come pick them up directly from you, but they do require coordination. Some items can be sold online, or through garage sales, although typically it's very difficult to sell things with enough speed and quantity to reduce clutter in a hoarded home. Giving items to other people that you know similarly tends not to move the needle much but is an option and can be helpful in some cases.

Bringing Openness and Values to Decluttering

As you do the practical work of discarding, think about how the other skills throughout this book can serve you. When your mind says that you can't let go of things that your mother gave you, or that it's too wasteful to put things in the trash, acknowledge the thought as a thought, and choose whether listening to it will serve you. Allow yourself to feel whatever emotions you feel about letting things go—the more you allow them, the more they will flow through you like a river going through a canyon rather than frothing up like whitewater rapids. Focus on what you are adding to your life by discarding items and making space in your home.

One client we worked with, Thomas, had been putting off decluttering for years after he inherited his parents' things when they passed.

He dreaded having to look through his father's mementos and confront how much he missed him. Figuring out his "why" made a huge difference—the big reason he wanted to declutter was so he could have space to invite his adult kids and their partners to his home and stay close to them as adults. As he connected with his values around family and hospitality, he felt that it was worth experiencing the sadness and grief involved in sorting through his parents' things. And while he did experience those emotions, he was also surprised by how much joy and satisfaction he took in sorting out their belongings, letting go of many items he didn't want to keep, and treasuring the select items he did.

Ways to Organize

Hoarded homes don't just have a lot of stuff in them, but the stuff is usually all mixed together without much rhyme or reason. Some people with hoarding problems have a great organizational system that's just buried under or behind too much stuff, but many have always struggled with organizing. If you're the latter type, you might have a box somewhere that contains expired food cans, newspaper clippings, your marriage license, and your spare cables. This makes it hard to find things when you do need them or to easily sort and put away things.

Categorize Your Things

As we touched on in chapter 4, the first step to organizing is to categorize your items, by function (items that you use on a task go together) or similarity (items that are alike go together). You can mix and match these systems too. Categories are most helpful when they aren't too huge, like 100 or more items, or too small, like 5 or less. The sweet spot for a category is often somewhere between ten and fifty items, but ultimately it depends on what works for you. For instance, if you're trying to organize clothing, "short-sleeved tops" or "work shirts" is more likely to be a helpful category than "all tops" or "plaid short-sleeved work shirts." Try to group things in one category together in the same location as best you can.

Give Them a Home

Ultimately, every item you own should have a "home" location where it belongs, and it helps if this can be intuitive to you and to other people. Usually, location should be based on putting a category together (e.g., all religious texts on the same bookcase) or putting items near where you use them (e.g., all coats on a rack by the front door). Once an item has a home location, try to put it back there each time you use it. As you declutter, think about the types of items you have and what they could reasonably be grouped with.

Again, aim for good-enough systems. Get all the stationery in one box near your desk for now. Maybe someday it can be separated into folders and notebooks and cards and placed in a desk drawer. For things that are hard to categorize, it's okay to have a "miscellaneous" category, but try to make sure that's a relatively small number of items, and to give them their own recognizable container or place. Putting items near where you use them when possible can be helpful. Adding labels can help a lot too, especially if you live with other people—we've never met two people who have the exact same intuition about where items "belong."

Create a Landing Zone

There are two areas that are especially important and deserve extra consideration. One is an in/out space. This is a place to put things that have just come into your home and need attention, like the mail or a medication you just picked up. It's also a place to put items that are leaving your home and need attending to, like a package you need to drop off. Depending on what works for you, this could be one place or a couple different bins. But make sure to give yourself a designated area for these items, and to look it over at least once a week and take care of the items inside. If you can handle something right away—like putting junk mail straight into the recycling bin—even better. But make sure you have a "landing zone" if needed.

Set Aside Important Documents

You should also have one place for your most important documents. Often, folks with hoarding feel like everything is important, so this isn't always easy to identify. But by most important documents, we mean the kinds of things that are really essential, like the thirty most important documents in your life that would be really hard to replace (e.g., car/mortgage documents, lease agreements, social security card or other identifying documents, this year's tax forms, etc.). If you have a more sophisticated system for organizing these documents that works for you, or you store them in a safe deposit box, that's great as well. But if you don't currently have a place for them, go find one container right now that you could put them in, label it, and start putting critically important documents there.

Ways to Acquire Less

If you have a lot of stuff coming into your home, cutting down on that will be crucially important to making progress and claiming your space. The world is more or less designed to make it easy for you to buy stuff these days. Every social media site is full of ads that are tailored to the things that catch your eye. As you drive around you, even in the most rural areas you likely see plenty of billboards and places you can spend money. You can buy with one click. You can subscribe and get new stuff automatically, forever. Life in the twenty-first century is wild. As we mentioned in chapter 6, setting commitments for yourself around not acquiring is likely to be important. Here are a few other strategies that can help you to bring down the influx of stuff.

Make Acquiring Harder

One strategy to try is increasing the friction between you and acquiring something new. If you know you'll be tempted to stop by a certain thrift store and you drive by it every day, find a new route to commute on. If you have your favorite online stores bookmarked, or items to buy bookmarked, delete those bookmarks. Delete your credit card info from your phone or browser memory. Delete apps and accounts that make it easy to buy things quickly. This isn't to say that you are helpless in the face of the thoughts and feelings that tell you to get stuff and thus you should avoid them at any cost. You can feel the urge to buy something, slow down, notice it, and make a different choice—this is a skill you're learning throughout this book. We just don't need to make this process harder than it already is.

We are all influenced by what we're exposed to. Make it easy to act in ways that align with your values and hard to act in ways that go against them. Putting time in between the impulse to acquire something and actually getting it can help take you off autopilot too. See something you like at the mall? Set a thirty-minute timer, and if you still want it then, make the purchase. Let the urge sit for just a bit and see what happens.

Practice Not Acquiring

Intentionally practicing not acquiring stuff can be helpful too. Choose a place where you normally feel compelled to buy things and go with a clear plan not to buy anything. Observe your thoughts and emotions and urges like a curious scientist. When you see something on sale, and your brain says you can't miss that deal, notice what an interesting thought that is. When your mind says that this specific cake pan would lead to an amazing, happy moment with your grandkids, recognize what a great storyteller your mind is. To set yourself up for success, the first time you do this you may want to bring a friend, or leave your money at home.

Track Your Successes

Keeping track of all the times when you want to acquire something and don't can be rewarding. If you have a paper calendar handy, put an X on each day that you saw something you wanted and didn't get it. Let those days add up, and appreciate how they move you in directions you want. Connect not getting things to the kind of life you want to live—one that has the physical and emotional space for whatever you care about most.

Get Your Joy Elsewhere

Getting something new can offer joy, excitement, and a sense of possibility. It makes sense to want that. Seeking out other sources of joy and reward can be really helpful so that acquiring things doesn't seem so compelling. Throw yourself into a hobby. Help a friend with a project. Take a walk around your neighborhood and see if you can spot a new plant blooming or a bird you've never seen before. Look for other things that can add to your life.

Flexibility and Faithfulness

Now that we've talked about more of the "what," let's revisit the "how" of decluttering. This is a book, and we don't know you personally, and we can't tell you exactly what will work best for you. So, honestly reflect on your past experience and your own abilities and limitations, and choose a couple strategies to try. Not all of them! Just a couple. One or two. Try them out, see what works, and adapt them to suit you. What works may change over time. Maybe right now you're in a phase of working three jobs to make ends meet, and the only thing you can really do is try some of the strategies to cut back on acquiring. Perhaps in another year you'll be able to drop down to one full-time job, and then you can dedicate several hours to discarding on your days off.

If a strategy doesn't work for you, try another one. If one stops working, set it aside. Treat this like an experiment and bring genuine curiosity. If you try something and it does, or doesn't, work for you, that's good information to have.

At the same time as you experiment, you also need to give a plan or strategy enough dedication and persistence to truly know if it worked for you. Some things take time to grow. A tree that doesn't grow leaves within the month of January isn't broken; it's a tree that needs time and sunlight and rain to continue growing.

We can't tell you exactly how much time to dedicate to any particular plan or strategy. As a rule of thumb, we'd suggest making a plan and following it with reasonable consistency and effort for three to six weeks before determining it isn't working for you. When you work on decluttering, look for "progress, not perfection." Ask yourself every couple weeks: Is what you're doing moving you in the right direction? Is there anything you could adjust to make it work better for you?

Barriers

It takes hard work and focus to recover from any hoarding problem, but there are factors that can make it extra challenging, including mental health struggles, disabilities of any kind, financial difficulties, social isolation, or lack of local resources. First, having another psychological condition like depression, ADHD, OCD, or post-traumatic stress disorder (PTSD), among others, may make it hard to declutter. If you have one or more of these conditions, you may find it particularly challenging to motivate yourself, to get started decluttering, and to sustain your focus and be consistent over time. You may also find the emotions around decluttering especially intense.

If you have a mental health condition that you think makes it particularly challenging for you to address hoarding, there are a few things we'd suggest. First, seeking help from a psychiatrist or psychologist or other licensed mental health professional may be highly beneficial if that's an option for you. There are also a lot of excellent self-help resources available these days: a couple you might consider are *Get Out of Your Mind and Into Your Life* (Hayes et al. 2005), *Things Might Go Terribly, Horribly Wrong* (Wilson and Dufrene 2010), and *The Mindfulness and Acceptance Workbook for Depression* (Strosahl and Robinson 2017). Work on taking care of yourself in the ways that are possible for you—things like getting enough sleep, exercising, or spending time in nature can all help you move in the right direction.

If the idea of addressing your home is overwhelming, give yourself permission to start small—really, really small. Pick a tiny area to work on or look for just five items you could let go of. Taking that first step often makes it so much easier to continue. If you have any supportive people in your life, try to let them in and make use of their support, whether it's to help you declutter or just someone you can text who will encourage you if you say you just let go of five things.

On the flip side, working on addressing your hoarding may help alleviate some of these symptoms too. One client we worked with, Patricia, had suffered with depression and hoarding for decades. When she looked around her home, it fed into feelings of guilt, shame, and worthlessness. In particular, she felt awful that her stove and sink were too covered with clutter to cook. When we started working together, her first goal was to clean off the stove so she could start cooking for her family again. After just an hour of sorting, she was able to use her stove and connect with something she really cared about for the first time in a long time, and her self-judgment and guilt started to become less intense, and easier to carry.

You may experience practical barriers too. Physical disability, medical conditions, and fatigue can all make decluttering more challenging. Financial difficulty can make it harder to declutter, as you may feel more pressure to get money "back" from your purchases or struggle with paying for gas to run items to other places. Similarly, if you don't have a car or can't drive, you may run into difficulty getting items out of your house.

We have a few thoughts on navigating these problems. None of these is a silver bullet, but it's worth exploring all your options to address barriers and make space in your home, and these strategies can make a big difference if you can put them in place. First, getting support from other people may be essential. We know how hard it can be to tell others about having a hoarding problem. Alternatively, maybe people in your life are well aware, but you've felt criticized or attacked by them over your things.

If there's someone who you think will support you with decluttering, we highly encourage you to reach out to them and explain how they can help. We'll go into more depth on this in chapter 9. Setting expectations (e.g., I want you to help me make decisions, or I just want your help taking bags to the landfill, or I want you to check in with me each Sunday and I'll tell you how much I've sorted) can make this much smoother. If it's possible for you, hiring professional organizers or home cleaners is one way to get additional support (we suggest seeking out those who have experience with hoarded homes specifically if possible).

If a lack of transportation is an issue, online groups where you can request that people pick up items may help you declutter even if you aren't able to drop things off. Again, you need a good-enough approach that works within what you are able to do. If you would prefer to bring old worn-out towels to an animal shelter, but it's not feasible for you to get to one, consider whether your values are better served by keeping the towels or putting them in the trash.

If you have ADHD or otherwise struggle with attention, focus, and time management, using alarms and visual reminders about decluttering, or scheduling decluttering in your calendar (ideally with reminders) may be beneficial. Russell Barkley's *Taking Charge of Adult ADHD* is a good self-help book to refer to for more specific strategies to manage ADHD. One thing to watch out for is the tendency for seeing an item to send you down a garden path where you find yourself starting a new project or remembering something else and don't end up focused on decluttering. Sometimes people with ADHD have the best intentions to declutter, but ten minutes after they tried to start decluttering, they find themselves repairing a lamp or downloading a new game without even remembering what they had meant to do.

This is just how some brains work—and these brains have lots of benefits too, like creativity and the ability to throw yourself into things. But in order to see progress in decluttering, we suggest working in one area or sorting through one box or bag and bringing your attention back to it repeatedly. You might try setting a timer on your phone for every five or ten minutes as a reminder to come back to decluttering if you've drifted away.

What if other people are a major source of your clutter? Perhaps you have clutter of your own, but you have a spouse who brings in even more stuff, or you have a mom who is constantly bringing over items that you don't want. We can't really do justice to the complicated topic of navigating relationships and stuff in this short space, but we'll offer a few starting points.

If a major cause of clutter in your life is other people offering or bringing you stuff, and you don't want the stuff, you have two options that can work: get comfortable saying no, or accept the stuff and then discard it as soon as possible. What will work best for you will depend on your relationship, but the choices basically narrow down to this. If you struggle to say a flat "no," it can be helpful to practice saying, "I'll think about it" or "I'll check and see if we could use it and get back to you."

When other people you live with add to the clutter, try to set realistic boundaries with them. Separate your spaces if possible (e.g., have a room or closet that is "yours" and clearly request that they not put any things in there). Ask them to keep specific spaces clear that would be most helpful to you (e.g., "I need the pathway to the door to be clear to feel comfortable. Please don't add anything to that pathway."). Try to make requests of them in a way that is specific, nonjudgmental, and communicates how their actions will help you (e.g., "Can you please go through the condiments and discard any that are expired or that you don't want anymore? It would really help me to have more space on that shelf so I can put the groceries away.")

What's Next?

The bad news is, there's no one perfect way to declutter or organize your space. The good news is, there's no one perfect way to declutter or organize your space, so you are free to experiment and see what works for *you*. In chapter 8, we're going to dive into an important topic: the connections between your belongings and your identity.

Another Brief Check-In

Now that you've read many of the chapters in this book, try checking in with yourself again. Here are a few questions to ponder (in your head, or by writing your answers down):

1. What have you learned that's been particularly helpful so far? What do you want to keep trying, practicing, or thinking about?
2. What strategies have you tried that weren't helpful? Why do you think they weren't helpful?
3. What progress have you made working on your hoarding? Even if it's small things, consider what changes you have made.
4. What do you want to keep working on?
5. Are there any barriers you've run into that have made it hard to work on your clutter? If so, are there any skills or strategies from this book that you might try to help address the barriers? Or other things you could try that might help you overcome them?

CHAPTER 8

Broadening Your Sense of Self

As you continue to work on organizing and decluttering your home and physical environment to meet your goals, you might find yourself struggling with an intense or maybe subtle nagging feeling. It might be the literal question "who am I without these things?" Or it might be a sense of loss from getting rid of certain objects, feeling empty or confused, doubting yourself, worrying about things being forgotten, and similar concerns.

One of the interesting things about being human is our ability to give deep meaning to experiences and even objects in our lives. Meaning is a rich word that ties in so many things—our values around what we do, but also how we see ourselves, relationships with other people, and our past experiences, and how we understand all of these things. Part of this is just what minds do—create and tell stories. But it's worth stopping to appreciate why. These stories give a sense of meaning to our life, helping us understand and make sense of our world, ourselves, and bringing purpose to what we do.

The Stories We Tell Ourselves

Because our minds are so good at telling stories and meaning is so important to us, we naturally include our possessions in this process. An old rocking chair could represent the time spent caring for a baby and that deep bond and love. Notes from school could feel like a connection back to exciting, interesting classes and the sense of self as someone who is creative, growing, and learning. In other words, our minds can tell such powerful stories about objects that they take on deep meaning and may even feel like a part of who we are.

All of that can be really beautiful and such a cool part of being human. We can have physical representations of our lives, meaning, and who we are. But, like many things about being human, it's a "double-edged sword" and if unchecked can create significant suffering.

Holding on too tightly to the stories of who we are and the physical manifestations of those stories can lock us into unhelpful patterns.

Consider for yourself what it has cost you to hold onto things because of what they mean to you. Maybe you haven't replaced items in your home, even if they are broken, because of what that object means to you. Maybe you've felt paralyzed to get rid of things because of a sense of responsibility to take care of important objects.

You might also have stories about yourself that make it hard to let go of objects. For example, "I'm a caring mother and it's my responsibility to save things for my child" or "I'm being wasteful unless I use things for as long as possible." Notice how these stories could have started by giving a sense of meaning to what you were doing, but over time they also can become more like a rigid rule you have to follow. If being a caring mother means you save everything for your child, what does it mean when you get rid of something? The stories we tell and the meaning we make about ourselves and our objects can sometimes become a rigid, dominating narrative that pushes us away from our own goals and values.

Finding Meaning Here and Now

Part of why we describe values the way we do in this book comes back to these issues with meaning. If you recall, we specifically talk about values in terms of finding meaning in the ways you act (like being kind, creative, or adventurous), rather than your possessions, the goals you achieve, what other people think of you, or how you think or feel about yourself. In particular, overly attaching meaning to possessions puts your values outside of the way you act and the person you are, making it instead about what you have, what you've saved, and what isn't lost or broken. You may even find that in an effort to save meaningful objects, you actually are taken away from being the kind of person you want to be and your values.

There's a natural tension inside all of this because it's uncomfortable to find meaning in the moments of our life that come and go. We strive to have accomplished or acquired meaning so we can feel safe in it always being there. It's comforting to attach to and keep the meaning we get. But consider: what if meaning is something constantly being built, experienced, and enacted in our lives? In the same way, what it means to be you is more in your ongoing experience of your life, rather than the stories your mind tells about who you are.

For example, you might find yourself storing books you read years ago as a way to hold onto what you've learned and as a way to represent parts of your identity and what has been important to you over the years. Judith held onto fantasy and sci-fi books that had allowed her to disappear into other worlds and that resonated with her sense of herself as an imaginative person and voracious reader. Marco had years of magazines piled up from the different hobbies he had gotten into, from models to fishing, and they fit with his sense of pride and expertise in all the different things he could do.

It might feel as if saving these books will help you save the experience and memory you had with each of them, and even deeper, saving these parts of your identity and who you were at different times in your life. Even if now, they are just taking up space in a closet and you know deep down you'll never read them again.

Realistically, you'll read books and learn things, and some of that you will remember, and other things will fall away over time. Yet, the meaning of reading and learning in that moment was there and you can continue to experience meaning with new books and learning new things. Our mind wants to hold onto each meaningful moment and keep it forever, which is fine and what minds do, but can be a problem when that gets in the way of you continuing to have more meaningful moments in your life. We want you to have the space and opportunity to keep having meaningful moments reading new things, rather than feeling overwhelmed in holding onto past moments and experiences in your possessions.

In this chapter we will explore a deeper sense of yourself that we hope can help empower you to be more open to how you approach meaning in your life, especially with your possessions. This sense of self is more like the steady foundation from which you experience your life moment by moment, finding meaning in how you live life now and the paths you continue to take. Connecting with this deeper, observing sense of self can naturally help you get unstuck from attachments to past stories about yourself and objects.

Paint on the Canvas

You can think of your experiences in your life as paint on a canvas. Major and small events are each their own unique brushstrokes that add parts to the painting. Some brushstrokes fade over time and new brushstrokes are always appearing, meaning this painting is constantly shifting. There are parts of the painting that feel really important, maybe relationships with people that really matter to you, and as you keep having new experiences, those parts of the painting continue to get added to, painted over, and otherwise change. There are likely really painful and upsetting parts to the painting too, that you wish you could paint over. Some might be right at the center of the painting and others might have faded over time. Overall, there is so much meaning in this painting about who you are and your life, and it keeps changing as you live.

The question is *Who are you in this metaphor?*

You might say you are the painting itself, and in some ways that's true. The collection of all your experiences is in some ways who you are. Just like this painting, you are always changing as a result of what happens in your life. But this level of self also comes with a lot of challenges. If you really are this painting, then what does it mean if an important part starts to get painted over or fades? How much effort, time, and focus has to go to maintaining the painting you want, keeping the stories and meaning alive and at the forefront? And can you really keep the painting the same over time?

Striving to keep the painting the way it is might even lead to it getting further away from what you want over time. It's hard to balance the brushstrokes and images that keep getting added while keeping other parts the same. The whole painting process might become more of an imitation of past brushstrokes, trying to keep things the same and recreate the past.

Just like a painting constantly being painted over, your life story is constantly evolving and changing. You might feel a pull to prevent that change, for example, by holding onto possessions that are connected to the past and the story of who you are. It can feel really scary to risk losing parts of yourself and your stories, including with the objects that carry so much meaning and history. If you really are the painting, then of course you have to do whatever you can to preserve it and protect the meaningful parts of your life.

What if there is a different version of you in this metaphor though? What if in some ways you are the canvas? Of course the canvas is part of the painting, but unlike the painting itself, the canvas never truly changes. The canvas is always there, being added to and being the container for everything that happens. We don't usually judge a painting based on the canvas it is on, but in some ways that's the point. You as the canvas isn't something to judge or tell a simple story about in terms of its value and meaning.

Also the canvas can just be there, experiencing and absorbing each meaningful brushstroke, without a sense of attachment of what should be there, what should be changed, what needs to be preserved, and so on. No matter what changes in the painting, the canvas is still there, unchanging and simply soaking up all that happens.

This deeper, more stable sense of self as the canvas can be useful to drop into at times like when things feel overwhelming, when struggling with change, and when you feel stuck in your attachments to the stories of who you are and the meaning of objects you've preserved. If you don't connect with this idea of a painting, other similar ideas may work, like "You are the sky and your thoughts and feelings are the weather that passes through," or "You are a chessboard and your experiences are like the pieces on the board." The idea is that you are more than and simply contain all of your experiences, including your thoughts and feelings as well as the stories about who you are and your possessions.

Connecting with a Deeper Sense of Self

This might feel a bit confusing. In fact, it should be confusing in some ways. Your mind likes to tell stories, including about who you are, and we are trying to go past that point with your mind. Try to instead notice the you that simply notices these stories. As soon as your mind starts telling a story to codify that deeper self, then in some ways you lose contact with that deeper sense of self. You shift from being the canvas to looking at the painting.

It's like how a flashlight can't illuminate itself—the you behind your eyes observing everything is a perspective to connect with rather than to tell stories about. See if you can be open to sticking with any confusion that comes up, noticing the urge to try to make sense of it intellectually, and instead bring a curious perspective to try to connect with this as an experience.

The best way to learn about this deeper self is by experiencing it. So let's try an exercise to help you connect with this deeper sense of self.

EXERCISE: Notice the Stories About Your Possessions

One way to think about what we are discussing in this chapter is attachment. Objects can have power in the meaning we give them, but more importantly, we give objects power when we get highly attached to them as representations of this meaning. In other words, people can get stuck when they hold on too tightly and rigidly to the meaning of too many objects that are essential to preserve. In the painting metaphor, this is like trying to save a part of the painting and prevent it from being painted over, which strains and affects everything else in trying to paint around it. Let's start to explore what attachments you have with some of your possessions.

After you read through these instructions, we will ask you to walk through a room in your house to notice your attachments (the meaning and stories that you give to objects and how strongly/rigidly you hold onto it). We are not asking for you to get rid of all of these objects, but just to notice the stories you give to these possessions and the attachment that shows up to hold onto this meaning.

1. Pick a room you want to walk around and explore in your home. Start with a room that is. less overwhelming and where you feel open to considering your attachments.

2. Walk around the room for about five minutes, and scan over different possessions that you see.

3. As you look at your possessions, notice when stories come into your awareness from your mind—about what these possessions mean to you, what they represent, and why they are important. Check in with how attached you are to this story—that is, how

strongly you are pulled to preserve and protect this story, like trying to keep a part of the "painting" from changing. Don't judge the attachment or story; this is just about noticing your reactions to objects and what your mind does.

4. For each object that you find a story for, see if you can pause for just a moment to notice "I am not this object." Literally say this to yourself out loud. And as you do, try to get in touch with the you that is the "canvas," the deeper sense of yourself that is observing this object.

5. Briefly consider to yourself, "Does this object still serve my goals and values?" Take a moment to consider whether holding onto this object is making your life feel fuller and more meaningful and able to do the things you want—or is there is a heaviness associated with the object (like stress, dread, guilt, etc.)? Does the object gets in the way of your daily life and what you do or does the object prevent you from getting something that works better and may make life easier?

6. Then move on to another object in the room. Continue this exercise for about five minutes. If you get fixated on one object, notice that, and then move on. If you have the urge to keep doing this exercise with every object or for a long time, acknowledge that, and make a conscious effort to end the exercise after five to ten minutes.

Go ahead and give this exercise a try right now. Then return to the book.

What did you notice doing this exercise? If you haven't done it yet, go ahead and complete it before reading on. Then take a moment to reflect on how this exercise went. Consider what stories and objects you found yourself strongly attached to. How does this story align or not with your values? Were several objects linked to the same story?

Were there any objects you've been preserving for a long time that had stories you weren't as attached to anymore? Maybe it was an old story that doesn't fit as much with who you are and what matters to you now. It's interesting how we can get attached to preserving even stories that aren't that meaningful to us anymore.

Notice too how you are not these objects, or even these stories, at one level. As the canvas, you simply hold all of these experiences, stories, and sources of meaning. Some objects are representations of what matters to you and your stories, but they are only representations insofar as you give that to them. That is great when being attached to an object meets your goals and values, but it's important to also notice when these attachments are causing distress and problems.

Were there any objects that you had a mixed reaction to? Maybe you wish you could get rid of it but also feel like you can't because of what the object means. Maybe it's overwhelming. Or it might be unhelpful to save because it's broken or doesn't serve its purpose anymore. Notice if preserving some of these objects is taking you away from your goals and values at this point in your life.

EXERCISE: Letting Go of Attachment

Are you willing to let go of some of these attachments to objects and stories about yourself, in the service of your goals and values related to decluttering? If so, then let's work on a goal to help you practice letting go of attachments. This means holding the stories and meaning of objects more lightly and challenging the need to keep these objects (and the stories they represent) as if they *are* what gives your life meaning. This doesn't mean getting rid of all of your meaningful possessions. It does mean noticing when your attachments to objects are no longer serving you in terms of your goals and values.

This exercise is really important in showing yourself that you are not your stories and challenging the unhelpful attachments your mind gives to your possessions. The more you practice letting go of these attachments, the freer you might feel to declutter and make choices that fit your goals and values. This way you will have the ability to choose which objects you keep without feeling weighed down by the stories you *have* to preserve. Being more intentional on the items we save to represent meaningful things can also make those remaining items and preserved stories more special and in line with your values. Most importantly, we want to help empower you to be able to let go of the objects that are no longer serving you and the stories that hold you back from where you want to be in life.

First, let's pick an object you are willing to discard that would show you that you can let go of attachments. You might pick an object from the last exercise, or you could pick something different. The idea would be to pick something that you feel an attachment to because of what it means to you and the stories of who you are. Also, the object should be something that no longer is serving you—for example it is broken, you have similar reminders, the story is not important or relevant in your life anymore or is not one that fits your current life and values, or the object is causing other problems.

Second, go ahead and take some time to just notice the stories related to this object. Watch how your mind gives the object so much importance and meaning with the stories it tells. See if you can also observe the pull of attachment to this object because of these stories. From that deeper sense of self, see if you can simply notice what your mind and feelings do as you consider the meaning given to the object.

Third, take a moment to recognize that you are not this story or this object. Just like the canvas isn't a brushstroke. These things can give you a sense of meaning, but it's also okay for them to change. You are still you, even as your life changes, the stories change, and as objects come and go.

Finally, go ahead and discard the object in whatever way makes sense. As you do, continue to just observe what your mind does and what comes up with your thoughts and feelings. You might be surprised by the pain that shows up, the worry that you have to go back and save this "part of yourself" or your story, feelings of guilt and responsibility, and so on. All of that is okay and a part of letting go of attachment. It's painful and you can choose to feel that pain in the service of your goals and values.

See if you can just stay in touch with whatever shows up, using the skills you've learned in this book to make space for your experiences, without them pushing you around. You might make a commitment to spend five to ten minutes just being with whatever shows up, while not acting on it. See if you can bring kindness to yourself in the process—it's painful to let go of attachments, and it makes sense to feel however you feel. Doing so actually empowers you to continue to get control over your life and your possessions, so you can be even more intentional about the meaning and stories you hold onto.

Self-Critical Stories

This chapter has focused primarily on the stories from our mind that have to do with attachments to possessions and the meaning they represent. Another type of story we want to call out briefly before we end is the self-critical ones. Our minds pick up all sorts of stories as we navigate the world in terms of who we are and why we do what we do. Some of these stories can be quite critical. They may include stigmatizing messages about hoarding, or other judgments and criticisms, and other painful stories about who you are. Once your mind has picked up a story, it tends to stick around, especially if it fits in with other negative stories that your mind has picked up over years. In some cases you can trace a self-judgment back to times you heard it from others (like being teased, a stigmatizing show about hoarding, or criticisms from family).

Your mind will pick up negative stories you hear and will start to apply them to you, becoming your own worst critic. The hard part of this critic is that it's with you all of the time, and it's always got a negative story to remind you of your failings and shortcomings, and framing things that happen in your life in terms of these criticisms.

Just like we explored letting go of attachments to the stories about your possessions, you can use the skills in this book to practice identifying and letting go of self-critical stories. The first step is to notice when your mind starts to jump in with a self-critical story. As we've talked about before, just noticing what your mind is doing takes away some of the power of these stories as you start to see them just for what they are: stories your mind has picked up over the years and likes to repeat and apply to you.

Once you notice these self-critical stories, you might use some of the strategies from earlier chapters, especially chapter 5. For example, you might practice labeling the thought (*I'm having the thought that people don't like me*), noticing what this story pulls for you to do, and whether acting on this thought fits or not with your goals and values. It's easier to loosen your attachment to these negative self-stories when you can get in contact with a deeper sense of self—that sense of "self as the canvas."

If you are reading this book because a loved one has a hoarding problem, we also encourage you to follow the same process to practice noticing the stories you have about your loved one. The stories we hold about our loved ones may also come from of a variety of sources, from our direct interactions to our own internal experiences to broader social attitudes we've been exposed to. Try noticing the thoughts you have about your loved one and their hoarding problem, and notice what those thoughts pull you to do. Consider the values that you hold toward your loved one and more broadly.

What's Next?

We hope this chapter helped you to gain a different perspective on how you approach the meaning your mind gives to your possessions and, more broadly, the stories your mind tells about you and your life. We encourage you to practice noticing stories about your possessions and letting go of your attachments to these stories and objects. Once you meet your goal of letting go of attachments to one object, take some time to reflect on how it went, and consider setting a new goal to practice with another object.

Next, we're going to explore the impact of hoarding on your relationships. We'll also share some ideas on how to build relationships that fit with your values and how to communicate effectively with your loved ones.

SECTION 3

Moving Forward

CHAPTER 9

Cultivating What Matters

In chapter 3, we introduced values and asked you identify your values. Bring two or three of them to mind: What do you want to have more space for—literally and metaphorically—in your life? The thing about values is we need to keep coming back to them. Even though it seems like values should be intuitive, they have a way of getting obscured by our fears or falling by the wayside when we get busy with life, no matter how important they are to us. In other words, values—or more precisely, valuing—is an active, intentional process. Which is why we return to values again here.

Values and Relationships

Now that you have your values in mind, consider how you could enact those values in your relationships. If your value is readily connected to relationships, like *growth*, this may be an easy exercise. For instance, you could ask yourself how you would like to grow as a parent, friend, sibling, partner, and so on. What lessons would you like to learn from and implement? What is the next step on your journey to becoming a wiser you?

If the value that came to mind was less obviously linked to relationships—let's say it's *beauty*—this part may take some deliberation. However, because values are qualities of being—they're about *how* you approach life and less about what you do—they are usually relevant to most domains. Thinking about *beauty*, you could brainstorm what an aesthetically pleasing relationship would look like—be creative! No one gets to define your values for you. For instance, you may define beauty in terms of how you interact with the other person, rather than the look of things. So, an aesthetically pleasing relationship could refer to using kind and thoughtful language, not sarcasm or passive aggression, or doing nice gestures for others without expecting anything in return, or creating a welcoming space in your home. Values are an excellent way to flex your creative muscles.

How Hoarding Affects Relationships

The reason we are focusing on relationships here is that hoarding can have a major impact on them. Not only does the distress associated with hoarding affect how we interact with people, but the stuff accumulated over time invariably affects those you share a space with—be it someone living with or visiting you. Here are a few ways we've seen hoarding impact interpersonal relationships:

- Disagreements about what to do with belongings leading to relationship conflict.
- Interactions with loved ones primarily revolve around items, stripping relationships of their nuance.
- There is miscommunication regarding the motivation behind hoarding.
- If loved ones don't understand why letting go of items is so difficult for you, they may feel as if you are "choosing" possessions over them and feel neglected.
- Shame related to clutter makes it difficult for you to invite people over, leading to a sense of isolation, loneliness, or self-loathing.
- Loved ones feel like they need to walk on eggshells around you, compromising the quality and closeness of relationships.

- Distress related to hoarding leads to either inadvertently overburdening loved ones by relying on them for emotional support or isolation due to worries about sharing emotional struggles.
- Clutter causes emotional stress for the people living with you due to lack of space and physical freedom—or even people who no longer live with you due to the strain it has imposed on your relationships.
- Clutter leads to hygiene issues for people in your home due to inability to clean difficult-to-access spaces.
- Excessive buying can cause financial strain, which may result in stress on others if you rely on them for financial support.

How hoarding impacts relationships differs across people, but you might be able to relate to at least a couple of the examples we listed previously. Indeed, hoarding sometimes affects relationships in ways you might not even realize, simply because hoarding has become a natural part of your life—in the same way that we might not realize how our mannerisms impact our interactions because we don't think of them as separate from who we are.

EXERCISE: Reflect on Your Relationships

To evaluate how hoarding has impacted your relationships, identify at least three specific ways hoarding or the emotions associated with your belongings have shaped your relationships. If you are struggling to answer this, think about what your partner, child, parent, or friend might say about your relationship. Maybe taking their position might help you see some ways in which hoarding affects your relationships. This step is important for building awareness and reckoning with the cost of hoarding with respect to your relationships, as painful as it might be, so don't skip it. Hurt and values are two sides of the same coin. You wouldn't care about relationship strain if you didn't value your relationships, and without acknowledging disconnection from values, it's difficult to work on connecting with them again.

Building Values-Consistent Relationships

Once you've identified the ways that hoarding has affected your relationships, consider what you want to be different about them. Sometimes it's helpful to start from the end point and work backward. When thinking about changes you would like to make to your relationships, rather than focusing on what you're doing "wrong," ask yourself how you want to show up in your relationships. Which values are most relevant? What would acting on those values look like in each of your key relationships? Be creative. If you have *sharing family traditions and history* as a value, you might choose to share stories about some of your belongings with your children (and grandchildren) before letting go of them. If you care about *staying healthy*, you might ask neighbors to go on walks with you or join a group class.

Remember that valuing is about *how,* not what, so focus on the *process* of showing up in your relationships (e.g., actively showing interest in the other person's life) rather than the outcomes you want to achieve (e.g., my child will visit me every week). One reason to care about the process is that it's much more under our direct control. For instance, when Judith started working with us on decluttering, she felt frustrated that her wife didn't appreciate or acknowledge her progress. But the more she focused on how she herself wanted to act (being more present and helpful to her wife), the more satisfaction she got out of decluttering and the easier it was to continue.

Of course, ideally, we would also like to be able to dictate the quality of our relationships—perhaps that our partner will be more enthusiastic about doing chores or that our child will be less energetic around bedtime—but you and we all know from experience that it's a fruitless struggle. In fact, we usually find that the more we push, the more we get pushback.

If you're feeling stuck on where to start, we have a few ideas. Use them only insofar as they align with your values and goals. They're not meant to be prescriptive or the "correct" way of doing things. You might even try some of them out just to see how they work for you and adjust accordingly.

Collaborate with loved ones on setting goals informed by shared values, especially if they're living with you. For example, both of you might have the value of *having a neat living space*, so that could be a starting point for a discussion on what that would realistically look like and what needs to change to get there. The crux of building on shared values is that both of your perspectives are being considered and you're starting from a place of what matters, rather than what the other person is doing wrong.

In addition, make sure you set clear expectations for what each of you is willing and unwilling to do. For instance, you might say that ultimatums are off the table, and you expect bilateral agreement on whatever next steps are taken. Your loved one might set an expectation for a minimum amount of clutter that needs to be reduced weekly. If any disagreements arise, it might be helpful to remind each other of the shared value your suggestions are coming from. That is, as hard as it may be to think about letting go of X number of items a week, connecting with the rationale behind that—to create a neat living space for yourself and your loved one—might make that pain worth it.

Communicate your needs and boundaries effectively. Too often, we assume that others know our intentions or what we're thinking without us having to say them out loud. Sometimes that is true, but when it isn't, making our thought process explicit can be incredibly helpful for getting the other person on the same page, especially because it gives context for where your request is coming from. This could mean being clear about the situation to which you're responding/referring in the first place and how it has impacted or is impacting you. For example, in chapter 2 when Judith was frustrated with her wife pushing her to declutter, she used to say, "Stop asking me to throw things away," and both she and her wife would end up feeling resentful and stuck. With practice, she started saying, "When you ask me multiple times to throw my things away on the same day, I feel ashamed and guilty, which makes me want to avoid the task entirely." This increased her wife's understanding and helped both of them communicate more about their options.

We also encourage you to describe what you need, rather than what you don't need. Continuing from the previous example, Judith found it helpful to ask, "Could you give me five minutes to reset?" It's always easier for people to follow directions about what to do than what to not do, which leaves an infinite number of possibilities for what they could be doing instead. When describing your request or boundary, be sure to provide objective details, so that there won't be any confusion about what you're asking for. In this example, if you ask for "some time to reset," you could mean thirty minutes and the other person could assume you mean five minutes, and this miscommunication could lead to a new argument.

As a cherry on top, tell the other person how listening to your request will help or benefit them in some way. Again, we expect people to understand why we're asking for what we're asking for because it's obvious to us, but in reality, it's tricky to know exactly what another person is thinking—no matter how close we are to them. Thus, Judith would end the discussion by saying, "After I have some time to reset, I'll be able to focus more on working through this pile of scarves." This helped Judith and her wife to both get what they needed from each other; Judith could work at the pace she was willing to take, and her wife got a commitment that Judith would keep decluttering.

The same strategy is useful when you're asking for help. Explain the problem you're facing, how it's affecting you, what specific help you need, and the positive consequences of you receiving help. For instance, you might say, "There are too many things we're working on right now and I'm feeling overwhelmed. Could you help me select ten or so items to start with to make things more manageable? Then we can start to work through things bit by bit together and I'll be able to stay focused."

When sharing your position or perspective, describe what others can realistically expect from you. Misalignment on such expectations is another potential source of conflict. For example, it may be helpful to explicitly state that it is unrealistic to expect you to bring a room full of items to the dumpster tomorrow. At the same time, set realistic but meaningful expectations for yourself, which means pushing yourself to do difficult things that are within your ability and let others hold you accountable to those expectations. As you might be able to tell from this section, transparency is crucial.

Show compassion toward yourself and others. The skills we've provided in this book are intended not just to help reduce clutter but more broadly to change your relationship with yourself and your thoughts and feelings. Part of changing your relationship with yourself is taking a more compassionate stance toward you. This means being able to show yourself grace and forgiveness when you make mistakes. It means letting go of the critical self-talk and recognizing that you're not alone in your human struggles. It means letting yourself take up space and deeply connect with other people, even if your mind says you don't deserve to. Clarify what self-kindness looks like for you, in your unique situation. Self-kindness can involve different behaviors, from giving yourself time to rest, to encouraging yourself to do hard things, to taking care of your basic needs through nutrition or hygiene. When we treat ourselves more kindly, it becomes easier to accept kindness and love from others.

Compassion also extends beyond the self. When we say being compassionate toward others, we don't mean being nice or polite. We mean taking the other person's perspective and trying to see where they're coming from, genuinely validating their experiences, and unconditionally accepting who they are. This doesn't mean condoning behaviors but empathizing with why someone did what they did, even if you disagree with their actions.

For instance, if someone took it upon themselves to bring your donation pile to the donation center without your permission, make the effort to understand why they did what they did. Why do you think they want you to reduce clutter or to change your habits? You can still ask them not to do that again (see previous section), but showing them empathy will help you let go of your frustration and anger more easily and provide an opportunity for connection instead of conflict. Perhaps they haven't extended that empathy to you, so it's difficult for you to take the first step—that's totally fair and understandable. This is where we return to values. What kind of person do you want to be in your relationships? What would that person do in this situation?

If you're reading this from the perspective of a someone whose loved one is struggling with hoarding, we would give you the same spiel. Take the time to reflect on their perspective. Try to understand why they are persisting in hoarding, even if you wouldn't do the same thing. If letting go of their belongings was easy, you wouldn't be here reading this book, and they wouldn't still be struggling. There must be something that makes letting go of items exceedingly difficult, so much so that they continue to hoard despite negative consequences and relationship fractures. Reflect on what that could be. In fact, you might have been in a similar situation to them at some point: have you ever continued doing something despite clear negative consequences? If so, use your experience to channel some empathy for your loved one. You don't need to understand them 100 percent, but it might help to make kind assumptions and relate to their pain however you can.

Ask for support outside your relationship. You may need to seek help outside your relationship to address issues in your relationship. There's no rule that you need to solve your problems by yourself, and most of the time, that's a tall order. If it's within your ability, find a mental health professional who can guide you through some of your relationship struggles. You might even seek couples or family therapy. Having a "neutral" party to provide support as you and your loved ones work through interpersonal friction can make a huge difference.

Expand connections. If you are someone who feels lonely or socially isolated, keep in mind that you are not alone—this is something common to many of the people we work with who have hoarding problems. It's not always easy to develop new relationships, but it can be done. Look for groups that fit with your interests, such as local clubs and meet-ups, recreational sports, game nights, churches, or volunteering organizations. Join online groups, particularly ones that are connected to your local area so they could lead to in-person connections. If you have one close friend, ask if they'd be up for introducing you to their other friends. If you meet people through your work or other avenues, and you feel like you get along, be willing to make the first step and suggest doing something together. If you have friends you've drifted away from over time, consider reaching back out—most of us underrate how much distant friends will enjoy hearing from us (Liu et al. 2023).

Develop relationships outside hoarding. As we mentioned earlier, one of the possible consequences of hoarding is that your relationships end up revolving around it. Your conversations are about when you will discard items, the reason you talk in the first place is to make plans around discarding, and so on. As you work on your existing relationships, it may also be helpful to find new relationships outside of hoarding. For example, you could rediscover hobbies, like finding a book club, connect with your neighbors by bringing over treats, or join classes in your community to meet new people. Doing so may also remind you that you exist outside your belongings and that there is a rich life waiting for you once you make space for it.

What's Next?

We're coming to the end of this book, with just one chapter left. As we've mentioned, the path of decluttering a hoarded home isn't always linear. There are lots of obstacles that can come up, and you are a human, not a discarding machine, so sometimes you'll falter in your progress and need to catch yourself and recommit. In the last chapter, we're going to talk about how to keep moving in the right direction over time.

CHAPTER 10

Walking the Walk

As you've worked through the skills and content of this book, we hope you now find yourself in a different place from where you started—somewhere closer to your goals and more in line with your values. At the same time, you're still on your journey. Indeed, most of us are on our own never-ending journey because that is the nature of life. So, before we end the book, we wanted to return to the topic of following through on goals, sticking to your valued course, and how to find your way back when you inevitably get lost.

As a brief refresher, remember that we used the acronym SMART for setting goals: specific, measurable, achievable, relevant, and time-based. The reason we care about SMART goals is they are step one to setting yourself up for success. Imagine if your goal was, "clean my house." It would feel like there was no end in sight, because who knows what counts as clean anyway? Moreover, you would likely feel immediately overwhelmed and unmotivated in the face of such a lofty goal.

This is a common mistake people make with their New Year's resolutions. They go big—stop drinking alcohol, exercise for one hour every day, complete a new home project once a month—and usually give up on their goals by March. To be clear, the mistake here is not setting such a goal per se. For example, if a person had a three-year plan to give up alcohol entirely, that might be feasible. It's the cold turkey or all-or-nothing approach that is a problem. So, keep your goals SMART and you will be more likely to get them done.

Committed Action

Once you have your identified goals (which is perhaps half the battle), you need to follow through on them. It's a harsh reality that all our intentions to change don't count for much until we translate them into action. Here, we don't mean *any* action. After all, we act all the time. For example, you might have sorted through some of your things this week, or called someone you haven't talked to in a while, or gone to the store to buy cleaning supplies. You do things as part of your daily routine. We call the kind of actions we're referring to, the ones linked to your SMART goals, as "committed action." The name might be a bit on the nose, but it's helpful to remember that there's an element of commitment and intentionality entailed in these actions.

How do you know you're engaging in committed action? First, committed action is tied to your values. So, things that you do in service of your chosen values will usually fall under committed action. Because of that, committed action is inherently approach-based and experienced as rewarding in some way, even if it's not fun.

For example, declining social invitations because you don't want to have conversations about your home situation is avoidance, whereas declining social invitations to stay at home and engage in a crafts project in line with your value of creativity is approach. In the first example, you're avoiding conversations, and in the second example, you're approaching a certain activity. Even though it looks the same (i.e., you're staying at home), the intention behind these decisions is different.

Second, committed action is behavioral. As such, it has a clear end point, unlike values. For instance, decluttering for thirty minutes or discarding ten items is a discrete behavior, and you're done with it at the end of thirty minutes or after ten items. Whereas, maintaining a calming living space is a value that will never be "done." You get to continue working on it throughout your life. As much as committed action is specific and accomplishable, it doesn't have to be observable.

That is, committed action may be intangible. If you're practicing observing thoughts about why you need to save items without acting on them, that's a committed action. Same if you're practicing mindfully orienting to something important in the present while your clutter beckons you to worry about it. As long as you're choosing to take these steps intentionally toward your values, they count as committed action.

Third, committed action feels *different* from most other behaviors. We recognize this is not an objective way to define committed action, but living your life according to your values is a subjective experience. What your version of a valued life feels like is different from someone else's version of a valued life. Or, even if it is the same experience, we wouldn't be able to tell—just how we can't ever know if two people experience the color blue in the same way.

So, we can't tell you what your valued life is going to feel like. You might experience more joy and meaning, you might feel more motivated to do things, you might feel more connected with your humanity, but ultimately, it's your unique experience to create and live out. Still, we can definitively say that it will feel *different* from what you have been doing, particularly if your life has been ruled by avoidance and rule following.

That is, if most of your life has been about trying to get away from negative consequences or aversive situations, committed action will feel different. If the reason for most of your behaviors is "it's always been that way," or "because I'm not the kind of person who does that," or "because that's how things work," committed action will also feel different from that. Committed action is you choosing what you want your life to be about through the actions you take, minute to minute, hour to hour, day to day, and eventually over many years. If you want a quick way to check if you're engaging in committed action, ask yourself, "Would I like to do more of this in my life, even if I won't always enjoy it?" If your answer is yes, then you're probably on track.

Staying the Course

As much as committed action changes how you experience your life, establishing this new habit requires relearning—for many—decades of behavioral patterns. Like any new habit, however, if you repeat it often enough, it'll start to become automatic. But, getting there is the challenge. So let's get this out of the way: you're going to fail. At some point, you will return to old habits, falling back into avoidance and rule following. This has nothing to do with lack of willpower or weakness; it has everything to do with being human. Now that we've set the expectation that you will fail sooner or later, we can make a realistic plan for how to stay or get back on track.

We need to approach committed action with a helpful mindset. Sometimes clinicians differentiate between a lapse (momentary faltering) and relapse (returning to problem baseline). A lapse is not the end of the world, and you can probably course correct by yourself. A relapse might require a higher level of intervention (e.g., talking to your therapist), although neither is the end of the world.

An analogy for distinction is driving from one end of the country to the other. Let's say you got caught up in a scintillating conversation and missed a turn. Do you say, "Oh well, guess we'll just have to live in Florida (or insert local city name here) now!" Or do you let your GPS recalculate your route and find your way back to wherever you were heading? The latter is what we want you to do if you miss a turn or take a wrong turn.

We get distracted by things all the time, and if you drive long enough, you're bound to go off course at some point—that's the expectation. So, take your missed turn in stride. Take a breath, let go of any "I should've…" or "If only…," and find your way back to your values. Similarly, notice any self-criticism or blame showing up and let it go; neither will serve you here. Remember, you're playing the long game, so in the grand scheme of things, one missed turn is insignificant. There are also things you can do to minimize your chances of veering off course in the first place.

Learn Your Triggers

It helps to know your triggers. When we say triggers, we mean situations, stimuli, or stressors that are likely to push you toward old patterns. For example, items that were used by your children might be triggers, in that they are especially hard for you to let go of, even if you're able to effectively use skills to let go of other types of belongings.

You might also notice that your urge to buy things goes up whenever you get into an argument with someone, so interpersonal conflict might be a trigger. For many people, general stress is a trigger. Even something like your neighbor blasting music at three in the morning, which in theory has nothing to do with hoarding, could be a trigger. Figure out what yours are by paying attention to what comes before the behaviors you're trying to change.

Once you have a sense of your triggers, you can take preventative action. Triggers mean that you are likely to fall into old habits, typically because you're more emotionally or mentally taxed, leaving you with fewer resources to engage in new responses. However, knowing that you're vulnerable is helpful because it means that you can do something to remedy the situation. For example, you might preemptively do something to manage your stress, like taking a walk, talking to someone, or reading a book, when you're at a five out of ten, rather than wait for it to go up to eight, when you have even fewer resources at your disposal.

If the trigger is certain groups of items, you could also arrange for a supportive person to be present when you're disposing of those items, to buffer the additional distress. If you're the kind of person who knows what it's like to get grumpy when you're hungry, this is akin to being able to recognize when you're hungry and irritable, and grabbing a snack before interacting with another human.

Watch for Warning Signs

Recognize your warning signs. These are cues that let you know you are beginning to get off course. Maybe it's running over the rumble strips along the highway shoulder or realizing that you haven't heard your GPS say anything in the past few minutes. Everyone has their own set of warning signs, so you'll need to curate your own personalized list, but here are a few examples:

- Mail piling up on the kitchen counter
- Chaos drawer starting to overflow
- Skipping or procrastinating decluttering appointments
- Skipping or procrastinating trips to the donation center
- Having to move things out of the way to do daily activities
- Leaving items on the floor for more than a few days

When you notice your warning signs, stay alert and intervene early before change feels overwhelming. Just like you may pull over at a rest stop to catch a nap or stretch your legs, we encourage you to return to the skills you've found helpful (from this book or elsewhere) and work on those muscles. For example, dedicate thirty minutes to sorting through your mail or commit to putting five items in the donation bin a week. Get in early before your molehill of items becomes a mountain of items, and follow the same principles for making sustainable change: set SMART goals and start small.

Focus on Consistency

Strive to be consistent. Training new habits is much like learning a new sport or language. Repetition is key, especially when you're not just learning new patterns but relearning what to do with familiar stimuli, like thoughts and feelings. In a way, it might almost be easier if you were totally starting from scratch, but you are working with years' worth of inertia. Because it's about consistency, try to practice a little bit every day rather than a lot once a week (or if it works better for you, once a week at a predictable time rather than once a month).

For example, if your weekly goal is to bring ten items out of your home, aim for one to two each day instead of waiting until Saturday and doing all ten at once. If you happen to be on a roll and get to ten on your first day, we still recommend continuing to get rid of at least one item a day for the rest of the week to capitalize on your momentum. You're shooting for long-term consistency, not short-term gains; generating sustainable change and converting new behaviors into automatic habits take time. Therefore, if you miss a couple days, that's okay. If you miss a couple months, that might be a warning sign.

Take One Step at a Time

Related to being consistent, take things step by step. Zooming out and referencing the big picture with values can be instructive from time to time, but in the moment, it can be more useful to focus on putting one foot in front of the other. If thinking about decluttering your living room feels unmanageable, focus on the area around the couch. If that feels like too much, focus on a side table. If that's also too much, focus on just one item. Compare your reaction to decluttering your entire living room to discarding one item in your living room. Which one are you more motivated to do? Just like a beach is made up of millions of sand particles, your life is made up of all these seemingly small choices over time. With each step you make, you are working toward building an oasis for yourself. A step is a step, no matter how small.

Stay Accountable

Develop a system for accountability. This could be a weekly check-in with your therapist, a family member, or even yourself. Figure out what helps you stay on track. At minimum, this system should have a method of tracking whether you've met your goals, so that you can celebrate your wins and troubleshoot any misses. For instance, you could reflect on what kept you from meeting your goals (e.g., logistical barriers, difficulty implementing skills) and make plans to navigate those barriers in the future.

However, if you notice that the reflecting is becoming rumination and self-blame, take a step back. Accountability is not meant to be punitive. Rather, your accountability system should reinforce your progress and keep you focused on your values-based goals. If you decide to recruit someone to support your accountability, make sure it's someone you can trust to be fair and supportive. For example, you don't want someone who subtly shames you if you don't complete your goals or makes you feel guilty for not setting bigger goals. You might even establish guidelines with this person, so that both of you are aware of your boundaries ahead of time.

Ask for Support

Ask for help when you need it. That's it. Being attuned to your triggers and warning signs may help you decide when to ask for help, but ultimately, you need to ask for it. Other people won't always know if you're struggling or if you want their help, and there's no shame in acknowledging that you can't do everything by yourself—that's not how humans were designed anyway. If you don't have supportive relationships, feel isolated, or aren't willing to talk about your hoarding problem with others in person, seek out healthy online communities with other people working to address their hoarding, and ask for help there.

Learn from Success

Finally, understand your successes. As we mentioned, straying from the course is to be expected, so when you do stay on course, it's worth reflecting on how you were able to accomplish that so you can replicate your successes the next time you find yourself in a tight spot. For instance, if you had a bad day and walked past one of your favorite stores and chose not to enter, reflect on what skills you used that enabled you to walk away. There is usually something you did (even if no one can see it)—these things don't just happen.

You might have noticed the urge and then let it be or disengaged from unhelpful thoughts about how buying a few more things isn't a big deal. Be curious about what you did and note these tried-and-true strategies. Because what works for others may not work for you and vice versa, we encourage you to identify the strategies that have specifically worked for you.

What Now?

With all that said, how do you proceed? Before you wrap up this book, ask yourself (again), *Where do I want to go from here? Where do I want to end up?* Whenever you feel lost or unsure, reorient to your values. They are your north star, so no matter where you are, as long as you find them, you won't be lost. Once you've identified the value you want to move toward, take that first tiny step—the tinier, the better. After all, you can only start from where you are.

References

Albert, U., D. De Cori, F. Barbaro, L. Fernández De La Cruz, A. E. Nordsletten, and D. Mataix-Cols. "Hoarding Disorder: A New Obsessive-Compulsive Related Disorder in DSM-5." *Journal of Psychopathology* 21, no. 4 (2015): 354–364.

American Psychiatric Association. *Diagnostic and Statistical Manual of Mental Disorders, Fifth edition, Text revision* (DSM-5-TR). Washington, DC: American Psychiatric Association, 2022.

Association for Contextual Behavioral Science. (2025, January 12). ACT Randomized Controlled Trials (1986 to present). Retrieved from https://contextualscience.org/act_randomized_controlled_trials_1986_to_present.

Ayers, C. R., M. E. Dozier, E. W. Twamley, S. Saxena, E. Granholm, T. L. Mayes, and J. L. Wetherell. "Cognitive Rehabilitation and Exposure/Sorting Therapy (CREST) for Hoarding Disorder in Older Adults: A Randomized Clinical Trial." *The Journal of Clinical Psychiatry* 79, no. 2 (2018): 3927.

Bates, S., A. J. De Leonardis, P. W. Corrigan, and G. S. Chasson. "Buried in Stigma: Experimental Investigation of the Impact of Hoarding Depictions in Reality Television on Public Perception." *Journal of Obsessive-Compulsive and Related Disorders* 26, 100538 (2020).

Beston, H. *The Outermost House: A Year of Life on the Great Beach of Cape Cod*. Macmillan, 2003.

Burkeman, O. *Four Thousand Weeks: Time Management for Mortals*. Farrar, Straus and Giroux, 2021.

Cath, D. C., K. Nizar, D. Boomsma, and C. A. Mathews. "Age-Specific Prevalence of Hoarding and Obsessive Compulsive Disorder: A Population-Based Study." *The American Journal of Geriatric Psychiatry* 25, no. 3 (2010): 245–255.

Chasson, G. S., A. A. Guy, S. Bates, and P. W. Corrigan. "They Aren't Like Me, They Are Bad, and They Are to Blame: A Theoretically Informed Study of Stigma of Hoarding Disorder and Obsessive-Compulsive Disorder." *Journal of Obsessive-Compulsive and Related Disorders* 16 (2018): 56–65.

Chia, K., D. S. Pasalich, D. B. Fassnacht, K. Ali, M. Kyrios, B. Maclean, and J. R. Grisham. "Interpersonal Attachment, Early Family Environment, and Trauma in Hoarding: A Systematic Review." *Clinical Psychology Review* 90, 102096 (2021).

Chou, C. Y., J. Y. Tsoh, M. Shumway, L. C. Smith, J. Chan, K. Delucchi, and C. A. Mathews. "Treating Hoarding Disorder with Compassion-Focused Therapy: A Pilot Study Examining Treatment Feasibility, Acceptability, and Exploring Treatment Effects." *British Journal of Clinical Psychology* 59, no.1 (2020): 1–21.

Dozier, M. E. *An Exploratory Investigation of a Standardized Exposure Task for Hoarding Disorder*. San Diego State University, 2019.

Fawcett, E. J., H. Power, and J. M. Fawcett. "Women Are at Greater Risk of OCD than Men: A Meta-Analytic Review of OCD Prevalence Worldwide." *The Journal of Clinical Psychiatry*, 81, no. 4 (2020): 13075. https://doi.org/10.4088/jcp.19r13085.

Fontenelle, L. F., J. E. Muhlbauer, L. Albertella, and J. Eppingstall. "Traumatic and Stressful Life Events in Hoarding: The Role of Loss and Deprivation." *European Journal of Psychotraumatology* 12, no.1 (2021): 1947002.

Frost, R. O., D. F. Tolin, and N. Maltby. "Insight-Related Challenges in the Treatment of Hoarding." *Cognitive and Behavioral Practice* 17, no. 4 (2010): 404–413.

Hayes, S. C. *Get Out of Your Mind and Into Your Life: The New Acceptance and Commitment Therapy*. New Harbinger Publications, 2005.

Hayes, S. C., K. G. Wilson, E. V. Gifford, V. M. Follette, and K. Strosahl. "Experiential Avoidance and Behavioral Disorders: A Functional Dimensional Approach to Diagnosis and Treatment." *Journal of Consulting and Clinical Psychology* 64, no. 6, (1996) 1152.

Kondo, M. *The Life-Changing Magic of Tidying Up: The Japanese Art of Decluttering and Organizing*. Ten Speed Press, 2014.

Krafft, J., M. E. Dozier, and A. C. Middleton. "A Preliminary Investigation of the Role of Psychological Processes in Hoarding Stigma." *Journal of Cognitive Psychotherapy* (2025). https://doi.org/10.1891/JCP-2024-0034.

Krafft, J., C. W. Ong, R. A. Cruz, M. P. Twohig, and M. E. Levin. "An Ecological Momentary Assessment Study Investigating the Function of Hoarding." *Behavior Therapy* 51, no. 5 (2020): 715–727.

Krafft, J., J. M. Petersen, C. W. Ong, M. P. Twohig, and M. E. Levin. "Making Space: A Randomized Waitlist-Controlled Trial of an Acceptance and Commitment Therapy Website for Hoarding." *Journal of Obsessive-Compulsive and Related Disorders* 39, 100846 (2023).

Kurtz, E., and K. Ketcham. *The Spirituality of Imperfection: Storytelling and the Search for Meaning*. Bantam, 1993.

Landau, D., A. C. Iervolino, A. Pertusa, S. Santo, S. Singh, and D. Mataix-Cols. "Stressful Life Events and Material Deprivation in Hoarding Disorder." *Journal of Anxiety Disorders* 25, no. 2 (2011): 192–202.

Levy, H., A. Naples, S. Collett, J. McPartland, and D. F. Tolin. "Central and Peripheral Physiological Responses to Decision Making in Hoarding Disorder." *International Journal of Psychophysiology: Official Journal of the International Organization of Psychophysiology* 205 (2024): 112437.

Liu, P. J., S. Rim, L. Min, and K. E. Min. "The Surprise of Reaching Out: Appreciated More than We Think." *Journal of Personality and Social Psychology* 124, no. 4 (2023): 754–771. https://doi.org/10.1037/pspi0000402.

Ong, C. W., J. Krafft, M. E. Levin, and M. P. Twohig. "An Examination of the Role of Psychological Inflexibility in Hoarding Using Multiple Mediator Models." *Journal of Cognitive Psychotherapy* 32, no. 2 (2018): 97–111. https://doi.org/10.1891/0889-8391.32.2.97.

Ong, C. W., J. Krafft, F. Panoussi, J. M. Petersen, M. E. Levin, and M. P. Twohig. "In-Person and Online-Delivered Acceptance and Commitment Therapy for Hoarding Disorder: A Multiple Baseline Study." *Journal of Contextual Behavioral Science* 20 (2021): 108–117.

Penzel, F. "Hoarding in History." In *The Oxford Handbook of Hoarding and Acquiring.* Oxford University Press, 2014: 6–16.

Postlethwaite, A., S. Kellett, and D. Mataix-Cols. "Prevalence of Hoarding Disorder: A Systematic Review and Meta-Analysis." *Journal of Affective Disorders, 256* (2019): 309-316. https://doi.org/10.1016/j.jad.2019.06.004.

Przeworski, A., N. Cain, and K. Dunbeck. "Traumatic Life Events in Individuals with Hoarding Symptoms, Obsessive-Compulsive Symptoms, and Comorbid Obsessive-Compulsive and Hoarding Symptoms." *Journal of Obsessive-Compulsive and Related Disorders 3*, no. 1 (2014): 52–59.

Rodgers, N., S. McDonald, and B. M. Wootton. "Cognitive Behavioral Therapy for Hoarding Disorder: An Updated Meta-Analysis." *Journal of Affective Disorders* 290 (2021): 128–135.

Ruscio, A. M., L. S. Hallion, C. C. Lim, et al. "Cross-Sectional Comparison of the Epidemiology of DSM-5 Generalized Anxiety Disorder Across the Globe." *JAMA Psychiatry* 74, no. 5 (2017): 465–475. https://doi.org/10.1001/jamapsychiatry.2017.0056.

Samuels, J. F., O. J. Bienvenu, M. A. Grados, et al. "Prevalence and Correlates of Hoarding Behavior in a Community-Based Sample." *Behaviour Research and Therapy* 46, no. 7 (2008): 836–844.

Strosahl, K. D., and P. J. Robinson. *The Mindfulness and Acceptance Workbook for Depression: Using Acceptance and Commitment Therapy to Move through Depression and Create a Life Worth Living.* New Harbinger Publications, 2017.

Stumpf, B. P., L. C. De Souza, M. S. Mourão, L. F. Rocha, and I. G. Barbosa. "Cognitive Impairment in Hoarding Disorder: A Systematic Review." *CNS Spectrums* 28, no. 3 (2023): 300–312.

Tolin, D. F. "Toward a Biopsychosocial Model of Hoarding Disorder." *Journal of Obsessive-Compulsive and Related Disorders, 36* (2023): 100775.

Tolin, D., R. O. Frost, and G. Steketee. *Buried in Treasures: Help for Compulsive Acquiring, Saving, and Hoarding.* Oxford University Press, 2013.

Tolin, D. F., S. A. Meunier, R. O. Frost, and G. Steketee. "Course of Compulsive Hoarding and Its Relationship to Life Events." *Depression and Anxiety* 27, no. 9 (2010): 829–838.

Tompkins, M. A., and T. L. Hartl. *Digging Out: Helping your Loved One Manage Clutter, Hoarding, and Compulsive Acquiring.* New Harbinger Publications, 2009.

Vogel, D. L., R. L. Bitman, J. H. Hammer, and N. G. Wade. "Is Stigma Internalized? The Longitudinal Impact of Public Stigma on Self-Stigma." *Journal of Counseling Psychology*, 60, no. 2 (2013): 311–316. https://doi.org/10.1037/a0031889.

Volker, J. M., and C. G. Thigpen. "Not Enough Parking, You Say? A Study of Garage Use and Parking Supply for Single-Family Homes in Sacramento and Implications for ADUs." *Journal of Transport and Land Use, 15*, no. 1 (2022): 183–206.

Walji, F., and P. Salkovskis. "Hoarding Disorder–Investigating the Relationship Between Reported Prior Deprivation and Current Beliefs about Fear of Material Deprivation." *Journal of Obsessive-Compulsive and Related Disorders*, 40 (2024): 100861.

Wheaton, M. G., L. E. Fabricant, N. C. Berman, and J. S. Abramowitz. "Experiential Avoidance in Individuals with Hoarding Disorder." *Cognitive Therapy and Research* 37 (2013): 779–785.

White, D. K. *Decluttering at the Speed of Life: Winning Your Never-Ending Battle with Stuff.* W Publishing Group, 2018.

Wilson, K., and T. DuFrene. *Things Might Go Terribly, Horribly Wrong: A Guide to Life Liberated from Anxiety.* New Harbinger Publications, 2010.

Yap, K., K. R. Timpano, S. Isemann, J. Svehla, and J. R. Grisham. "High Levels of Loneliness in People with Hoarding Disorder." *Journal of Obsessive-Compulsive and Related Disorders, 37* (2023): 100806.

Zakrzewski, J. J., R. Henderson, C. Archer, O. R. Vigil, S. Mackin, and C. A. Mathews. "Subjective Cognitive Complaints and Objective Cognitive Impairment in Hoarding Disorder." *Psychiatry Research, 307* (2022): 114331.

Jennifer Krafft, PhD, is an assistant professor at Mississippi State University whose work focuses on acceptance and commitment therapy (ACT), self-help, and hoarding. She is editor of a book on innovations in ACT, has received grant funding from the Association for Contextual Behavioral Science (ACBS), and has published thirty-five journal articles.

Clarissa W. Ong, PhD, is an assistant professor at the University of Louisville. She serves as associate editor for the *Journal of Contextual Behavioral Science*. She has published two ACT books; has contributed to more than seventy journal articles, including those on ACT, hoarding, and perfectionism; and has received grant funding from ACBS and the International OCD Foundation (IOCDF).

Michael E. Levin, PhD, is a professor at Utah State University. He is an ACBS fellow and past editor in chief of the *Journal of Contextual Behavioral Science*, the peer-reviewed ACBS journal. He is a leading researcher on developing, evaluating, and disseminating self-guided ACT interventions for a wide range of mental health concerns. He has conducted more than fifty clinical trials evaluating ACT self-help interventions, and has made several of these programs publicly available as part of the USU ACT Guide suite of services.

Michael P. Twohig, PhD, is a professor in the psychology department at Utah State University. He is a past president of ACBS. He has written more than 200 peer-reviewed publications and over ten books, and has received funding from many organizations, including the National Institute of Mental Health (NIMH).

Foreword writer **David F. Tolin, PhD**, is founder and director of the Anxiety Disorders Center and the Center for Cognitive Behavioral Therapy at the Hartford Hospital Institute of Living in Hartford, CT. He is author of *Face Your Fears* and *Doing CBT*.

Real change *is* possible

For more than fifty years, New Harbinger has published proven-effective self-help books and pioneering workbooks to help readers of all ages and backgrounds improve mental health and well-being, and achieve lasting personal growth. In addition, our spirituality books offer profound guidance for deepening awareness and cultivating healing, self-discovery, and fulfillment.

Founded by psychologist Matthew McKay and Patrick Fanning, New Harbinger is proud to be an independent, employee-owned company. Our books reflect our core values of integrity, innovation, commitment, sustainability, compassion, and trust. Written by leaders in the field and recommended by therapists worldwide, New Harbinger books are practical, accessible, and provide real tools for real change.